ENCRYPTED

A fresh look at God, how He functions and communicates.

By

E. G. Menzies

COPYRIGHT

ENDORSEMENTS

These are unprecedented days of restoration and reformation. God continues to raise up a company of men and women articulating "one sound," with one voice (2 Chronicles 5:13), heralding the glory of the Lord that is filling the earth. E. G. Menzies is such a voice.

As I read the original manuscript, it is with clarity and simplicity, that *Encrypted* has accurately and clearly unfolded the mind and plan of God for His people and Church.

In these days, Believers cannot be content with only attending church services, but we must seek to learn the wisdom from the sons of Issachar, in order to discern the times we live in. Let us take careful note of the Word of God, which cautions us that His people perish for a lack of knowledge. God is doing something dramatic and specific in our day and this book imparts powerful insights that help to understand more clearly what the Holy Spirit is doing in the global Church, and more specifically the individual Christian Believer.

When we read a good book on any subject, we cannot help but consider the significant research that went into its preparation. In reading this book *"Encrypted"*, I cannot help but consider not only its scholarship but also the experiences which E. G. Menzies has had, that incubated and sustained the necessity for penning such a book. It is my earnest prayer and expectation that this book will add to your life and be used by the Lord to bless and inspire you. May you be touched by Encrypted!

Michael Scantlebury, Apostle
Dominion-Life International Ministries [dominion-life.org]
Author of over 15 books

This book Encrypted, was written out of an in-depth relationship with God the Father, Jesus the Son, and the precious Holy Spirit. I have personally observed the author's walk, growth and intimacy with the Holy Spirit and it is from Him that the inspiration came for what has been written.

The call to intimacy originates in the very heart of God and it is to this that we have been chosen by our Lord. Encrypted seeks to capture the heart of the believer and inspire them to go deeper in God.

E.G. Menzies has endeavoured to convey the hidden riches contained in the Word of God and stir one's soul to the reality of an unsearchable God. Let "Encrypted" sharpen your senses and draw you closer to God.

Harry Dreher
Pastor, Overcoming Faith Centre, B.C., Canada

AUTHOR'S NOTE

I believe that you will find Encrypted thought provoking. You will find that it bears words that are like medicine for the soul, every dose is important. You may read quickly through the pages but chances are that you will find yourself returning to study each section, to ensure that the values of which you had a glimpse in your quick read, is captured by your mind and understood. I believe the information shared in Encrypted will strengthen you as a better person, in spirit, mind and body. As you read, do take time to check the scripture references to ensure you satisfy yourself that every principle expounded is based solidly on God's word. Encrypted not only reveals coded things of God but unveils many spiritual principles in simple language. My prayer is that you will be blessed and have a better appreciation of the true and living God, faith in him and the lifestyle which encompasses both.

ACKNOWLEDGEMENTS

Sincere thanks to editorial consultants Anita Cheek-ita and Pauline Osborne-Ellis, for their assistance. Thanks also to my family and friends for their support in so many ways while I worked on this book.

****

Translation of Cover Image: The dove depicts the Holy Spirit and He sheds light on the encrypted word to bring revelation to the believer.

Table of Contents

INTRODUCTION

If you believe in a higher power, no matter what others say, you must be clear about what you believe and how you define your God. You do not want to be the person serving a god who is a "runner-up" or serving him out of ignorance. Most of us will only direct our worship to the one we believe to be invincible and the supreme ruler of the universe. You take pride in knowing who you serve is not one among others, like another luxury car. He must be the God so great that He stands out in a class all by Himself; no other like Him, before or ever will be. He must be distinguished as the only God who is:

> ➢ Immutable and eternal – He will never change, in among other things, appearance, power, values, love, mercy and grace.
> ➢ Perfect and Just - He is therefore a God of truth, holy and completely without sin.
> ➢ Omnipresent – He is everywhere. Wherever you are God is there also. Whenever you need Him, He is there.
> ➢ Omnipotent – He must be all powerful. He can therefore do all things; nothing can be impossible or difficult for Him to do. He must be the creator of all things. All things must originate from him and all things must end with him.
> ➢ Omniscient – This God must know everything.
> ➢ Faithful – You can trust Him.
> ➢ Supernatural – He is spirit.
> ➢ He is alive and will always be - He can therefore speak, hear, feel and laugh. You can as such have a

relationship with him. He must be able to communicate with you and you with Him.

If you have discovered such a God, this book will tell you more about Him. If you have not met such a God, this book will introduce you to Him and so, to you this God declares:

> *[11] I know the plans I have for you, no one else does, plans of favour that will make you prosper and will not hurt you, plans to give you hope and a good future. [12] Then you will turn to me for help and come and pray to me, and I will listen to you and help you. [13] You will search for me and find me, when you have searched for me with all your heart. Jer. 29:11-13*

This book delves primarily into HOW the true and living God speaks to us as individuals and how we can speak to him. If you are a worshipper of the true and living God, then no matter what the denomination or organization, we all serve the same God. No one gets it all right from day one. There is a constant place for spiritual deepening, where we learn more about spiritual things to which we have already been introduced and for spiritual widening, where we continue to be exposed to new and greater truths about the God with whom we have been drawn into relationship. We must therefore be open to the Spirit of God to guide us into new dimensions, so that we may grow into a closer relationship, through a better understanding of God and that which concerns Him and His kingdom. It is with this background that "**ENCRYPTED**" has been written, from a place where it is just one person, you with God in the room; and He says, "Come, let us reason together" (Isaiah 1:18) .

A DESIRE FOR INTIMACY

Safe Conversation

Every human desires companionship, a close personal relationship with someone we can trust, truly trust. Some people may not admit their need for companionship as they may have become cynical about love, life and relationships in particular. For some people life experiences may have brought them to a place where now they believe, such a desire is naïve, and the indulgence of an innocent mind. Still, deeply, hidden somewhere at their core, is that wish to find such a relationship with a person with whom they can share their deepest thoughts, and know their secrets are safe. They want to have that close friend, mother or father, someone who will truly listen to them. They desire someone who will listen to all their fears and inhibitions without judgment, and knows how to gently guide them to a lighted pathway.

Sometimes you may feel, in your own daily experiences, as though you just want to cry out loud. You want to scream at the top of your lungs in those times when life grips at your gut with its wrenching claws. In those times, you also want to know you have someone in your corner with an understanding ear, or better yet, someone who knows what every sound means and who can provide healing to every wound, (or so it seems) just by having them listen. That is how it is for everyone, whether we admit it or not. The fact is that as old and experienced, big and strong, stoic and unflinching, confident and knowledgeable, beautiful and popular, famous and wealthy, wicked and nasty, worldly and wise as we sometimes are, life can find a way to bend us to the breaking point. If you have not been there yet, I guarantee your turn will come. We all find ourselves in those circumstances where we wish there was someone more caring than a mother, "more tender" than a lover, more forgiving than a priest, who would hold us and help us believe it is going to be alright.

As humans we have a tendency to often forget, and so the best things we have in life we sometimes fail to draw on, even when we need them desperately. We become overwhelmed with life and the kerfuffle involved in simply living, and so we often forget about helpful resources we have at our disposal. We forget like the lady who just lost her husband in a horrific accident. She has all kinds of expenses coming to her and she does not know where to turn to have them paid. She has forgotten about the insurance policy they bought to take care of things in the event this said circumstance should arise. She has forgotten it promises to cover such expenses within a matter of days and that a great deal of her headache could be gone with a simple call to the insurance company. Her emotions are now entangled and her mind cannot think straight, so she forgets. We also forget that we have someone who cares for us and to whom we can relate the way we deeply desire. He is available to all that call upon His name. The Apostle Peter admonished that we cast all that we worry about on Jesus because he cares for us (1Peter 5:7). Jesus himself said we can come to him if we labour and are heavy laden and he will give us rest (Matt 11:28), that he will not leave us without comfort (John 14:18). He will never leave us, nor forsake us (Heb 13:5) and that we will not find any greater love than his love for us, on account of which he gave his life for us (John 15:13).

Still, every now and then we find ourselves wondering: "Where is God now that I need Him? In the midst of all these who witness my circumstance, how do I talk to Him and know that only He knows the affairs of my heart as I speak? How can I communicate with Him, just Him, no neighbour in on our conversation, no devil and his angels eavesdropping to thwart my plan with Him. Can I send a message coded to God so that only He knows where I am at? Can God talk to me like that? Can our conversation be **ENCRYPTED?**

The Greater Dimension to Which We Aspire

"Encryption" is often used when sending messages or documents on the internet. In order to protect the contents of the document, you may encrypt it. Encryption allows only an authorized party to access or read the contents of your message using a private password. Without encryption, information is at risk of exposure to undesired people who may use or exploit it. This could lead to all kinds of situations, theft, embarrassment and even death. Encryption may seem new and modern to the average person, but is it really? We hear about the Internet and the various ways information is handled via the worldwide web. Is this all new? What is **NEW** really? Solomon who is deemed to be the wisest man to have ever lived wrote in Eccl 1:9-18,

⁹ The things which have been, will at some point cease but will come into being again. That which was done will be done again. There is nothing new under the sun.

¹⁰ Is there anything of which it can be truly established, this thing is new, it has never been done in any form before? It has all existed in some form before our time.¹¹ We do not remember the things that have been before and the things that are going to happen will not be remembered by those who come along later either. ¹² I am the Preacher; I have also been King over Israel in Jerusalem. ¹³ I have been zealous and put considerably resources into wisely researching all things done in this earth. This is the severe duty that God has given man, to work. ¹⁴ I have looked extensively at things done in this life, and frankly none of it makes sense, it is all frustrating and a waste of time. ¹⁵ The things that are crooked cannot be straightened and the things that are inadequate cannot be counted.

¹⁶ I contemplated in my spirit: I have accomplished a great deal. I have become wiser than all those that were before my time in Jerusalem. Yes, my life has been the exercise of great wisdom and knowledge. ¹⁷ I purposed in my heart to be wise, and also to experience great enthusiasm, excitement and foolishness. I see this is also perturbing. ¹⁸ For in much wisdom, is suffering, and the more you know the greater your pain.

Solomon in all his wisdom and after his many pursuits came to realize that we are locked in a cycle *("… this is the severe duty that God has given man, to work")*. Are the activities of life designed just to keep man busy?

What does it mean when the Bible says *"All things were made by him; and without him was not anything made that was made"* (John 1:3). Could it be that what we consider new are simply re-presentations of things old? Are man's "new" innovations really new, or do they just appear new?

Take the fashion industry for instance. In Genesis we see God as the first designer of clothing –*"Unto Adam also and to his wife did the Lord God make coats of skins, and clothed them"* (Gen 3:21).

The written word came forth as God set in place the practice of recording information. God did this when He gave Moses the law and the commandments that He had written on tablets of stone (Ex 24:12, Ex 34:1). Ancient scrolls of information or hieroglyphics etched in stone are being discovered time and again. There has been great advancement in information and technology. Interestingly, the more we learn about the past, the more we discover how we still know very little about what existed before us.

Eccl 3:11 notes:

> *God has made **all things** proper, suitable, appropriate or beautiful to suit its right time; **He has embedded in the consciousness of man a desire to know about eternal life, and has orchestrated things so that man will never be able to reason out or discover what He, God, has done from beginning to end.***

Also in Eccl 8:17

> *Then I observed and reflected on the work of God, no one can fathom the things that He has done in this world; even though people search hard to find out what God does, they still cannot discover or understand the extent of it, furthermore, though there are wise people who think they can figure it out, yet still they never will.*

In this twenty first century, scientists are discovering bones of animals which they estimate lived millions of years ago. We also know there are over forty seven calendars in use today. So, do we really know what year this is? The more we discover and advance, the more we learn that we know very little, we are sent in a whirl like a puppy trying to catch its tail.

In the 1967 academy award winning British drama "To Sir with Love", lead actor Sidney Poitier plays the role of a high school teacher. He invites his class of rowdy kids to visit a fine exhibition of "Costume through the Ages" at the Victoria and Albert Museum, as well as a visit to the Museum of Natural History. He points out to the students sporting trendy modern hairstyles, that in reality, their hairstyles were from 200 years prior and their clothing and dress styles were birthed in the roaring 20's. What was old is new again, again and again.

Three D movies are all the rage as people flock to see the movie of their choice in brilliant colours and with depth that makes you feel like you are a part of the set. The younger generation may think that this is all new technology, but fifty years ago, there was a popular item called a view-master that allowed the user to view colourful 3D images. The view-master was a novelty item invented in 1939 and popular through the 1970s. You could pick up a set of slides to remember the vistas you visited on your trips. It was like being there in person again. Most people born after 1980 would have no clue as to what a view-master is or even heard of the view-master or 3D photography. 3D movies are a direct result of the view-master invention. With this 3D movie trend we have seen a new rise of 3D photography and a resurgence of the View Master. If you think this 3D effect is all new, think again..., fifty years ago it was the craze for another generation of young kids.

Everything we say we have made is comprised of things that already exist. Everything old is new again. Did we truly invent something new or just re-introduce something old?

Brad a young father, came home from work one day and brought a small gift for his son David. Nothing expensive, just something to say, "I was thinking about you today". It was a tub of play dough. David was excited and immediately got to work fashioning all kinds of things from the dough. First he made a tiny table, then a chair and with what was left he made a little car, or so he thought. He ran to show Brad who congratulated him on his craftsmanship and told him how great they looked. By dinner time however, David had crumbled all the items he made and said he was going to make a new and bigger car like the one Dad drove. David created his car, table and chair based on his knowledge of them. He sat at a table, on a chair and would go for rides with his father Brad in what seemed to be a very big car.

So then, were the items he created new? Were they original? Was there original knowledge behind them? Was the material used new or recycled?

Here is what we know for sure:

David's creations were items made based on prior association with similar things on some level. He had seen, heard, touched, read or in some way been exposed to the concept of a table, chair and car.

His resources were limited to that which he had been given. His world of creations was therefore limited not only conceptually but also materially. David had therefore begun to recycle. So he crumpled his table, chair and car so he would be able to make a bigger car.

The boy refashioned his dough to reference his father, and the knowledge and lifestyle he had with his father. **Jesus did likewise as he tells us in John 5:19 that the things which he did were things he had seen his Father do, he also functioned out of prior association.**

> *"... Verily, verily, I say unto you, The Son can do nothing of himself, but what he seeth the Father do: for what things soever he doeth, these also doeth the Son likewise".* John 5:19

There is one true creator, God. All things are created by Him. He gives us the raw materials. We take the trees and we make paper of all kinds: toilet paper, writing paper, printing paper and so on. From trees we also garner lumber to make furniture of all kinds, tables, chairs, benches and the like. We at some point decide to throw them out and they go back to the soil, or some components to the air, from whence came all the things that helped to bring forth the tree in the first place. And a seed is planted, a seedling grows using the nutrients from the soil that came from the decomposed table or bench and using carbon dioxide from the air and so the cycle goes. What we have not seen in the cycle is new land created or new air.

There are many ways to look at things "new"; whether invented, recently made, discovered or noticed but here is the essential truth:

> **Our existence is within the absolute boundaries established by God. There is an invisible realm which bears the epitome of all human concepts. All things tangible have come from that invisible**

realm. We are constantly influenced by the invisible realm from which man came and carries a spiritual connection.

15 He is the image of the invisible God, the firstborn over all creation. 16 For by him all things were created: things in heaven and on earth, visible and invisible, whether thrones or powers or rulers or authorities; all things were created by him and for him. 17 He is before all things, and in him all things hold together (Col 1:15-17 NIV).

The invisible world is more real than that which is visible. All things visible come from the invisible realm.

Through faith we understand that the worlds were constructed by the word of God, so that things which are visible were not made from visible material, because they have been spoken into existence by the word of God. Heb 11:3

Our thoughts and ideas are ways that the invisible realm influences what becomes visible or tangible in our world.

The extent to which we can create from the thoughts and ideas we get is limited. We are limited by our level of understanding and commitment to the translation of those thoughts, but more significantly by the capacity with which God has endowed each person to create. The Bible says;

"As a man thinks in his heart so is he" (Pr 23:7), for thoughts become actions or things. We believe that we have infinite capacity to learn, create, develop and grow but even this is a matter that is relative. We may think we are unlimited in our ability to create, but God's scope is so much greater than we can imagine, a thousand years in His sight are as short as the passing of a day (Ps 90:4). *"...beloved, be not ignorant of this one thing, that one day is with the Lord as a thousand years, and a thousand years as one day"* (2 Peter 3:8).

> **As we create and build in this world, we are subconsciously seeking to advance a model here, of what our spirit knows already exist. Our spirit was there when God created all things. It continues to give us a glimpse of that which already exists in a dimension where our spirit was a part of God.**

There is a greater thing we seek. Man desires to go to the moon, but it is not really about a trip to the moon. Man's ultimate desire is to dwell in the heavens. Man has that association of dwelling somewhere quite different from earth. A part of man has been there before. This resulted from having a creator who gave of himself, and breathed life into clay so that man became a living soul. He placed His nature in mankind.

> **The deposit from God was not only air to bring forth life but also a composite of God's nature. This deposit from God activated mankind's body, soul and spirit.**

Now we as living beings made in the image of God also bear His creative trait. Within our limitations we constantly mimic concepts already perfected. Fundamental concepts of communication, transportation, clothing, shelter, food, art and defence are enshrined in a desire to model the conduct, lifestyle and environment out of which our spirit came.

In transportation we started out walking, we then progressed to riding on the backs of donkeys, horses and camels in order to go from one place to another. Next there were the boats and wheel carts. Fast forward to the present and we have every kind of motorized vehicle as well as airplanes which make intercontinental travel an everyday thing. The real pursuit in all of this transportation revolution is to efficiently move from one place to another when we wish to do so, and as quickly as possible. We have still not attained the ultimate travel mode which Jesus tapped into, whereby he could simply turn up where he needed or wanted to be:

And after eight days again his disciples were within, and Thomas with them: then came Jesus, the doors being shut, and stood in the midst, and said, Peace be unto you". John 20:26 *(see also* John 20:19, John 6:15-25*)*

Phillip, one of the twelve Apostles also had a similarly transcendent transport experience:

*[39] And when they were come up out of the water, the Spirit of the Lord caught away Philip, that the eunuch saw him no more: and he went on his way rejoicing. [40] But Philip was found at Azotus: and passing through he preached in all the cities, till he came to Caesarea. (*Acts 8:39-40*)*

We could talk for ages about God and His defence strategies to protect His people. At the end of the day we would still be left in bewilderment concerning how such things could be. For instance:

- He opens the Red Sea so His people can cross on dry land and then closes walls of water to drown the pursuing enemy (Ex 14:13-31).
- He sends His people to fight a battle by marching around the enemy's city blowing trumpets and shouting (Josh. 6:1-21).
- He sends his warrior into battle armed with only a sling and five stones (1Sam 17:31-58).
- He glorifies himself by trimming his army of thousands down to three hundred men, selecting who would fight based on those who lapped like a dog. (Judg. 7:1-25)

Yet He was victorious in every battle.

Who knows the ways of God, there is none like Him:

- He heals all manner of sickness and disease.(Matt 4:23)(Ps 103:2-6)
- By His spirit He gives the gift of healing to His people (1 Cor 12:9)
- By Him healing came through just a word or a touch (Luke 6:18-19) and (Matt 8:8-16)
- By the tree of life He made provision for the healing of the nations. He provides trees which He

plants on the banks of the river for food. The leaf of these trees shall not fade and shall be for medicine. (Ezek 47:12) and (Rev 22:2-3)

Greatest of all He made you and me, His perfect work of art. The loving, supreme Potter, carefully formed clay into his own image. He then placed His seal of approval, by breathing life into his creation, to make man complete, a living soul.

God has put in place all we need to fashion the things for our existence. And with his creation comes order for everything, including how we communicate with Him. Like a loving father bends his ears to listen to his young child, God listens to us closely, privately, just God and me, or just God and you. Yet, in an indescribable feat, He manages to accomplish this concurrently if needs be. He has an innate supernatural GPS-like ability and truly knows where each one of us is located.

In case you do not know what GPS is, I will elaborate. The GPS or Global Positioning System (also another concept attributed to being new), is a satellite based navigation system made up of about 27 satellites. The US Department of Defence has launched these devices into orbit. Though initially intended for military use, since the 1980's the system became available to everyone, anywhere in the world, at any time of day or night and in any weather condition.

Each GPS satellite orbits the earth two times daily in a precise manner and transmits signal information to earth. A GPS receiver, such as the one you may have in your cell phone or on your car dash, takes these signals and is able to calculate your exact location. Interesting, isn't it? Man has found a way to track the location of any user of a GPS device, no matter how many users, no matter where in the world.

Do you remember as a child being told to be careful what you say because God is listening? Do you remember being told how God knows where you are and sees everything that you do? The fact is; God knows everything about you. Far beyond the tracking of a GPS device, He knows your intentions, your secrets, your quiet thoughts and your outward actions.

> **God knows where you are, what you are thinking and what you are about to think and do.**

> **Is it possible that like a GPS user must have a receiver to be in communication with the GPS, a part of man's spirit is connected with God? Is it plausible that as a receiver, man's spirit transmits to God all that takes place with the individual?**

Some modern day truckers will tell you, that their truck is equipped with a GPS device. Their office can tell where they are and even how fast they are driving. The trucking company can shut a truck down if they decide to do so, whether the driver likes it or not. They can do this no matter how far away on a trip the truck might be. God knows everything about us. He can shut us down if He decides to, whether we like it or not. He knows where we are physically and spiritually. His advanced capabilities allow Him to see us with more accuracy, hear us and know even our thoughts from afar off. God's GPS operates from His throne in the heavens. While man's GPS system can only record what has occurred, God can also tell that which will occur.

A GPS device guides us to our desired destination via a route it plots that we should follow. God in a similar manner can guide us. He gives a [1]word of wisdom, a [2]word of knowledge or a [3]prophetic word to help us move ahead. With the GPS we do not have to follow where it guides us, so it is also with God, we are not compelled to follow his guidance, we have a choice.

In Psalm 139:1-10 David wrestled with the far reaching omniscience of God when he said:

[1] O Lord, thou hast searched me, and known me. [2] Thou knowest my downsitting and mine uprising, thou understandest my thought afar off. [3] Thou compassest my path and my lying down, and art acquainted with all my ways. [4] For there is not a word in my tongue, but, lo, O Lord, thou knowest it altogether. [5] Thou hast beset me behind and before, and laid thine hand upon me. [6] Such knowledge is too wonderful for me; it is high, I cannot

---

A word of wisdom, a word of knowledge and the gift of prophecy are spiritual gifts (1Cor 12:8).

[1] The word of wisdom is God's wisdom spiritually imparted to an individual so that they can proceed accurately concerning a matter.

[2] A word of knowledge is God spiritually imparting knowledge to an individual concerning past or present happenings or conditions.

[3] A prophetic word is a word from God communicated about the future to edify, exhort or encourage a person or group.

attain unto it. ⁷ Whither shall I go from thy spirit? or whither shall I flee from thy presence? ⁸ If I ascend up into heaven, thou art there: if I make my bed in hell, behold, thou art there. ⁹ If I take the wings of the morning, and dwell in the uttermost parts of the sea; ¹⁰ Even there shall thy hand lead me, and thy right hand shall hold me. (Ps 139:1-10)

The Bible declares so many truths to us and in the book of Jeremiah God himself highlights His GPS-like attribute:

Can any hide himself in secret places that I shall not see him? saith the Lord. Do not I fill heaven and earth? saith the Lord. Jer 23:24

So the Internet and GPS, like so many other things man has fashioned, may all seem new, but if we look closely enough we can see it is just a mere shadow of something that God already has in place. So far a shadow, that we cannot even see the thing is already there. Our eyes are too dim; our understanding too small. Our best imaginations cannot begin to conceive the dimension to which God has taken such a thing.

The Mind of God

As we explore our desire for intimacy there is an inevitable conclusion after all our searches. It is this, a certain level of trusting relationship and safe conversation can only be found in a relationship with God. It is then that we also understand that the greatness that our life's purpose enfolds is only accomplishable when God gives us insight. He will reveal His mind to us as we deepen our relationship with him. **Anything that we pursue in tandem with God guarantees optimality.** It does not mean that in the natural everything we do will be successful, but in the end the sum total of our quest will be optimal.

The issue therefore is whether we can exercise restraint and give God complete control to lead us.

An active personal Christian faith necessitates seeking God by studying His word. In carrying out our Christian duty we therefore seek the mind of God. Some people do believe that they have the mind of God, and in a sense yes. But in reality, can we think like God? Not really. In Isaiah 55 verse 9 God says: *"For as the heavens are higher than the earth, so are my ways higher than your ways and my thoughts than your thoughts"*, this has not changed and will not change. Paul in his writing to the Corinthian brethren explained:

"9 ...Eye hath not seen, nor ear heard, neither have entered into the heart of man, the things which God hath prepared for them that love him. 10 But God hath revealed them unto us by his Spirit: for the Spirit searcheth all things, yea, the deep things of God. 11 For what man knoweth the things of a man, save the spirit of man which is in him? even so the things of God knoweth no man, but the Spirit of God. 12Now we have received, not the spirit of the world, but the spirit which is of God; that we might know the things that are freely given to us of God. 13 Which things also we speak, not in the words which man's wisdom teacheth, but which the Holy Ghost teacheth; comparing spiritual things with

spiritual. ¹⁴ *But the natural man receiveth not the things of the Spirit of God: for they are foolishness unto him: neither can he know them, because they are spiritually discerned.* ¹⁵ *But he that is spiritual judgeth all things, yet he himself is judged of no man.* ¹⁶ *For who hath known the mind of the Lord, that he may instruct him? But we have the mind of Christ".* 1 Cor 2:9-16

Having the mind of Christ does not mean we know all that is in God's mind. Instead it means God gives us the privilege of sharing His thoughts about certain things. So He thinks as only He can think and shares His thought with us through His Holy Spirit, as we come into close relationship with Him. He desires that we come into oneness with Him through the knowledge of His **WORD**. Eventually, as does the Son and the Holy Spirit, we function in agreement with God's mind. In which case, we have the mind of Christ. For the knowledge of Jesus Christ is imparted to the believer (as we mature) through the **WORD** of God. Its understanding is taught to us by the Holy Spirit so that we can increasingly process things we encounter as Christ would.

"If you think the way I thought,
Where would be the mystery?
If you could do every miracle I
wrought,
What would be God about me?

I am God, all by myself God,
That's how it was,
That's how it is and always will be.
I am God all by myself God,
Trust in me and you will see.

by: E. G. Menzies

Nuggets - A Desire for Intimacy

1. We desire someone to trust.
2. Nothing is new.
3. There is an invisible realm which bears the epitome of all human concepts.
4. Our thoughts and ideas are ways that the invisible realm influences what becomes visible or tangible in our world.
5. As we create and build in this world, we are subconsciously seeking to advance a model here of what our spirit knows already exist.
6. There is a greater thing we seek.
7. We desire to model the conduct, lifestyle and environment out of which our spirit came.
8. God knows where you are, what you are thinking and what you are about to think and do.
9. God listens to us closely, privately, just God and me, or just God and you.
10. Anything that we pursue in tandem with God guarantees optimality.

THE ENCRYPTED WORD RECEIVED FROM GOD

Word Power

Language, whichever one you examine, has always had the handicap of limited scope for precise expression. In some languages one word is often used to convey numerous meanings. An English dictionary for instance will offer several meanings for just about any word you research. The term "**WORD**" as well as its biblical roots, in Greek: rhema[4] or logos[5] and in Hebrew: dabar[6], have not escaped the limitations of human inability to consistently convey a clear account of events or sentiments. When the term "**WORD**" is used in Christendom it usually refers to God's **WORD**, a divine expression from God to affect someone's life or affairs.

> In a more general sense however, whatever the term used for WORD, by whomever it is spoken and whatever the context, we must never miss

---

[4] Rhema (Greek) -the spoken word, an utterance or the thing of which is spoken.

[5] Logos (Greek) - the "Word of God" in substance or physical for example: Jesus Christ in the flesh.

[6] Dabar (Hebrew) - a "word event" or prophetic word. The term dabar is seen in the Bible as more than just the spoken word but refers to people and actions including the incarnation of Christ.

that every WORD (intangible) has the potential to become something of substance (that is, something that has significant effect, value or physical form).

A simplified analysis of the root word rhema, shows it consist of "rhe" (I say; I will say) that which is spoken and the suffix "ma" used to form noun from verbs. Therefore rhema is the **WORD** spoken but it also has potency to manifest in substantive form, a noun (person, place or thing), that is a form having practical measurable importance, value, or qualitative effect.

In the beginning was the word (logos) and the word (logos) was God and the word (logos) was with God. The term "logos" is usually used to represent the "Word of God" in substance or physical form, as was the case of Jesus Christ in the flesh. While rhema and logos are sometimes used interchangeably in the Bible, at the heart of the logos is that it represents the substance of an utterance. **I believe the term word or any of its root terms bears at the core that words have the power to transform.**

A word is like a seed, every seed has the potential for life, a physical form or something of evidential effect. A seed is typically not seen to be alive, but in essence it is alive and possesses the potential for great life attributes in it. Ironically a seed must die or rot (its circumstances removed) before it can bring forth life. The massive life potential within an acorn is only known when the seed has been nurtured through death to resurrected existence and manifest overtime to be a huge oak tree. Synonymously, **every word is destined to become substance.** Every word from God is intended to bring life or substance of one form or other. In <u>Luke chapter 1</u>, when the angel spoke to Mary the words [31] "thou shalt conceive in thy womb, and bring forth a son", Mary asked: [34]"how shall this be?" [35]The Holy Spirit shall come upon you and the POWER of God will overshadow you... the angel said, understanding what the words were meant to achieve, Mary then gave access: [38]"be it unto me according to thy word", that is to say, I choose that the substance of the word you have brought, be materialized in me.

We possess the capacity to encourage the development of words in order that they may manifest as the form for which they were intended. We also possess the capacity to neglect words and their intended end will never be realized. This is true of words spoken by humans and of even greater truth as regards words spoken by God. God's word can change anything or create anything. When it comes to humans however, because God has given us choice, there is a human responsibility. We must choose whether we welcome the change that God's word is meant to execute. We have that same power of choice regarding any word seen or heard, spoken by anyone, to us, around us or about us. **We decide if words affect us, the ability to do that is a God given power.**

When it comes to salvation the aforesaid principles also hold true, the seed (i.e. *the word* [logos] *of God.* Luke 8:11) is sowed by the preaching of the word and one is saved if:

A. one believes - done in the heart.

This is the nurturing process of words, where through thoughts, in the mind, words are brewed and one comes to terms with what has been said and decide whether one is convinced that it applies true or not. **Thoughts come from one of sources, God or the devil. A thought from the devil is referred to as a lie and is always a misconstrued or warped version of a truth, meant to achieve a reciprocal effect by way of deception. A thought from God is the presentation of God's word by the Holy Spirit to a person and is known as truth.** Whether or not words eventually manifest in one way or the other depends on how the recipient of the words responds. **The processing of the word is done in the mind and the distilled conviction is stored in the heart. We are admonished therefore to guard the mind.**

B. confesses the Lord Jesus Christ - with ones mouth.

Humans are created in the image and likeness of God and likewise have the power to speak and create or destroy. Proverbs chapter 18 verse 21 states: *"The tongue has the power of life and death..." NIV.* The one who speaks does not always control the end result concerning the words that are uttered because God has given everyone the power of choice in every matter concerning one's own life. However, when words are spoken the seed is sown to produce life or death. When we speak concerning words we have seen or heard we instil life or death into those words and thereby actualize that they flourish or die.

> **One's own words have more power over one's self, than do the words of anyone else.**

In the Bible, when the term word is used, particularly in relation to salvation, it often carries a condition: "if"

*"If ye abide in me, and my **words** abide in you, ye shall ask what ye will, and it shall be done unto you."* John 15:7

*"Then said Jesus to those Jews which believed on him, If ye continue in my **word**, then are ye my disciples indeed;"* John 8:31

"If" suggests there is a condition to be met for a relative result to follow. If I do something, then there is an effect that ensues. Understand therefore that:

1. **Words can do, only if I do...**
2. **Words have power but I have power over words.**
3. **Words I believe are empowered by what I speak.**

How does all this tie in with the purposeful word in the life of the believer? God's creative power is displayed in two ways:

1. God physically transforms his thought into substantial form as he did when he created man.

2. God creates substance by using words that carry the transformative potential to manifest the object of his thought.

In accordance, Jesus Christ was a word from heaven sent by God as a seed in Mary who nurtured and rebirth Jesus Christ in the form of flesh. One of the most significant applications of God's word is in the transformation of the life of those who believe in him. A believer is born again, not in the flesh but in their spirit through the instrumentality of God's Holy Spirit acting on his word sowed as a seed in the believer. (This conduct is similar to the Holy Spirit acting on the seed of the word Jesus Christ, sowed in Mary).

[9] *But ye are not in the flesh, but in the Spirit, if so be that the Spirit of God dwell in you. Now if any man have not the Spirit of Christ, he is none of his.* [10] *And if Christ be in you, the body is dead because of sin; but the Spirit is life because of righteousness.* Rom 8:9-10

Notice that Jesus who is the **WORD**, logos, (being the substance of all things embodied in God the Father) was spirit, born again into flesh. He still bore his substance, his spirit, which never changed; his form changed to flesh. Jesus was not the Logos because he became flesh. His spirit took on the form of man, flesh, and so he logos, the **WORD**, his substance now became clothed in flesh so he could dwell among men. It is not Jesus' flesh that made him logos; it is the fact that He possessed the fullness of God the father's mind, power and purity. His substance made him logos. When Jesus changed his form so he would dwell among men in the flesh, he did not change his substance he changed his form, how the substance would manifest. Jesus the WORD manifests in heaven as spirit. Jesus the **WORD** manifests on earth as flesh.

A basic science class in early years of school shows that H_2O the chemical formula for water can be in various forms: as a liquid, it is water, as a solid, it is ice, as a gas it is water vapour; its chemical composition or make-up, its substance does not change, it remains H_2O. The form of the matter H_2O, changes. The spirit of Jesus Christ took on the form of man so that he could dwell among men, thus he became Jesus (logos) in flesh. Water is transformed to ice (solid) if it must exist in a freezer, and is transformed to vapour (gas) if it must exist in the air. This is an established pattern concerning substance and form; it is the way God has things worked out. There is nothing new under the sun!

Man must be born again not so that our form will change but so that our substance, our spirit is changed. We cannot change ourselves. Our attempts to change attitudes, habits, conduct and the like is futile, merely superficial. When God changes a person the change takes place in the heart, the core of our being, a change of substance, a spiritual change. It is a God principle *"...First clean the inside of the cup and dish, and then the outside also will be clean."* Matt 23:26 *NIV.* Our mortal bodies cannot ascend into heaven, our spirits will. Everything to do with the eternal kingdom of God must first be transacted in the spiritual realm. We can only walk in the benefits of God's kingdom when we understand that transactions are done in the spiritual realm and can then be manifested in the natural not the other way around.

God's word can transform anything or be transformed into anything he desires. In the beginning we have accounts of God's spoken word transformed to substance: "let there be light, let there be a firmament in the midst of the waters, let the earth bring forth grass, all instances where the spoken words became substance, logos. Words are tools, agents with the power to change for good or evil.

Logos is dynamic, it can change its substantive form. Like heat aids in the "trans-<u>form</u>-ation" of water to vapour or of ice to liquid. God's word is the "trans-<u>form</u>-ative" agent in the life of a person. God's word will change your substantive form.

The believer is transformed by the word of God and is born again and begins the process of becoming the word (logos). [7]"The image of the Son of God, into which true Christians are transformed, is likeness not only to the heavenly body, but also to the most holy and blessed state of mind, which Christ possesses."

The essence of the believer there and then becomes his spirit. Just as the essence of Jesus Christ was not his flesh but his spirit. He was Christ the spirit dwelling among men in the flesh; his substance remained spirit. So Jesus says to you the believer, fear not him who can kill the body, but him who can kill both body and spirit because for the believer, just as with Jesus, the essence of the person is the substance, the spirit that dwells in the flesh. That which is born of the spirit is spirit and that which is born of the flesh is flesh.

Therefore, God keeps giving the believer life changing words, not so that we can change from the flesh to spirit, we will be in the flesh until we die or Christ returns, but in the meantime the word comes to continuously transform our spirit to be like God, in spirit, mind and power. Our substance must change and conform to God's similitude.

---

[7] Thayer and Smith. "Greek Lexicon entry for Eikon". "The NAS New Testament Greek Lexicon". . 1999. - Public domain. http://www.biblestudytools.com/lexicons/greek/nas/eikon.html

The Purposeful Word

Have you ever thought that God's word is coded? A word specifically designated for you where you are at this point in time. Why is it you may be in a congregation and a spoken word, heard by everyone has a particular meaning to you **NOW**? Maybe you have even heard it said before, but **NOW** it seems so much more powerful; so much more relevant. Why does a scripture read many times, all of a sudden pop out and these particular words seemingly leap from the text at you? You may have even memorized these words and can recite them at the drop of a hat, but **NOW** it is all different, all new. Perhaps no one else in the room sees what you see there, or understands it the way you do right **NOW**. Why is that?

Why would God not reveal His complete word to everyone when it is read? Why would it not be understood in its fullness? Does God have fun keeping us in the dark? Is the concept of Heaven a carrot on a stick and we need to continually be in pursuit of it, never attaining it? Well Lord, what do you have to say for yourself?

Au contraire (on the contrary), the Bible states: *"Thy word is a lamp unto my feet and a light unto my path"* (Ps 119:105).Therefore, we know God does not desire to keep us in the dark.*[4]In him was life; and the life was the light of men. [5]And the light* (or **WORD**) *shineth in darkness; and the darkness comprehended it not* (John1:4-5). We know also, that we do not have the capacity to comprehend God in His totality. So we cannot process the **WORD** in totality. Even the disciples were not privy to everything. As stated in the following excerpt of scripture Jesus once speaking to the disciples said:

*[12] I have yet many things to say unto you, but ye cannot bear them now. [13] Howbeit when he, the Spirit of truth, is come, he will guide you into all truth: for he shall not speak of himself; but whatsoever he shall hear, that shall he speak: and he will shew you things to come (*John 16:12-13*).*

God desires His **WORD** to be with us always. I believe He wants us to have a relationship with His **WORD** as it was in the beginning. You see *"In the beginning was the Word, and the Word was with God, and the Word was God. The same was in the beginning with God" (*John 1:1-2*).* God desires all His relationships to attain this standard, where we become His **WORD**; just as Jesus is the **WORD**.

Consider this scenario; when a family takes a young girl to live with them, she will grow and will take on traits and mannerisms exhibited by this family. Her eating habits, work ethic, and her tendencies will mirror those of her host family. No matter how long she lives with the family however, she will always know that she is not really a part of that family, if for nothing else, because she bears a different name.

The host family decides to adopt her formally and she is given the family name as her own. She now belongs to and with a family that loves her. The relationship is stronger and no matter what, she is family because she bears the name and has the documentation to prove it. Your name helps to define you as a person. She is no longer "Jane living with the Smiths." She is "Jane Smith", daughter of Mr. and Mrs. Smith and sister to several offspring of the family. The Smith family stamp is upon her.

Likewise, the stamp of God's **WORD** defines us as one with him. **This is what He is after, that we become the WORD and dwell with him.**

God therefore gives us His **WORD** for a purpose at hand so we can process and apply it as we walk. Consequently, daily transforming us to become like Him, the **WORD**.

"10 For as the rain cometh down, and the snow from heaven, and returneth not thither, but watereth the earth, and market it bring forth and bud, that it may give seed to the sower, and bread to the eater:11 So shall my word be that goeth forth out of my mouth: it shall not return unto me void, but it shall accomplish that which I please, and it shall prosper in the thing whereto I sent it" (Isa 55:10-11).

Every word spoken by God is designed to accomplish a very specific **THING**. It will not be spoken out of season, and God does not jest. When He gives us a word, it is designed to accomplish something specific which will bring glory to Him.

Think about it. If you had someone in your life who tells you everything of value they can impart to you all in one conversation, would you be inclined to enjoy talking to that person anymore? There would be nothing new to your conversation and nothing else of value in which to engage, so you would likely avoid that person. Further conversations would be an utter waste of time unless you wished to indulge in mere frivolity. We usually engage in conversation to derive something. It may be entertainment, counsel, instruction, but there is a desired end. If you have a mentor however, or someone with whom you are in close relationship, you consult with that person from time to time, in order to obtain counsel on a matter so you can execute a particular **THING** with wisdom.

When God gives us His WORD, it is a crafted WORD designed to accomplish a particular THING.

Similarly, Jesus, the **WORD** made flesh; when he was sent, he was sent into the world to accomplish a specific **THING**. He would bring salvation to man. Further, as Jesus was sent into the world to accomplish a particular **THING**, so were we. No potter makes a vessel, having no clue for what it can be used. The potter has an intention the moment he starts to design the vessel.

The potter's intent may be to create something that may be utilitarian or decorative, but he has something in mind. Likewise, God the supreme potter did not create us without a distinct purpose in mind. We all have a purpose, the end of that purpose we know, is to bring God pleasure.

Cognizance has to be given to the fact that we can only accomplish that purpose, that **THING** for which God has placed us in this world, when we come into alignment with God's word for our lives.

As His vessels, in order to know His intent for our lives we must consult the Master Potter, only He knows our true purpose. A wine decanter may make a beautiful vase, but is that its true purpose?

God's word is so powerful that when he speaks to us it demands much of our mental capacity to grasp that which he imparts. His thoughts are higher than our thoughts. We must therefore process what God imparts to us in a moment and apply it to our lives as He instructs. Doing so enables us to grow to know and understand Him more. The potter knows about the clay used for each vessel. He knows what we are made of better than we know ourselves. He knows where the scares are and what is needed to heal them. He knows for the purpose He has in mind for this vessel, it must go through a certain degree of heat or testing and must endure such for a given time. **God knows what you must take so that you will not break.** He carefully selected the raw materials and crafted every detail to entrench all that is intrinsic to the functionality, whilst accentuating the desired character of each vessel.

The WORD is ENCRYPTED (put into code or altered using a secret code so as to be unintelligible to unauthorized parties). The Bible, God's WORD is always available to us but we see in part and like the Apostle Paul says (1Cor 13:9) we know in part. The Holy Spirit reveals or decodes for us as required to accomplish each thing in our lives until that which is perfect is come and that which is in part is done away, all in accordance with God the Master Potter's plan. That is awesome!

Jesus was on earth to accomplish a specific **THING,** but he had to leave. He was only here on a mission. When Jesus was about to leave the earth, he said the Holy Spirit will come, "whom the Father will send in my name". Ummh, what does that mean? We know that Jesus is referred to by numerous names, among such he is known as the WORD. This implies that the Holy Spirit can also be called the "**WORD**"? ......and He shall teach you all things. Therefore, **all things**, even the things that God gives us a **WORD** to do, the Holy Spirit will come to enable us to accomplish them. Well, well, isn't that something? So even though God gives us a **WORD** to accomplish a **THING,** we cannot accomplish that **THING** unless the Holy Spirit imparts the knowledge or skill and helps us understand how it may be done. The Holy Spirit must decode the word from God to us in order that we may execute it because we cannot understand it on our own, it is **encrypted!**

The Holy Spirit will come, "whom the Father will send in my name". In the beginning was the **WORD** Jesus Christ. His name is **WORD**. *For there are three that bear record in heaven, the Father, the WORD, and the Holy Ghost: and these three are one (*1 John 5:7*)*. When God speaks His words are spirit and life. The Holy Spirit comes to us as **WORD**. Jesus is **WORD** and the Father is also **WORD**. All dwell together as one, one spirit, one word, one God. All are one. God sends us the Holy Spirit who is **WORD** so that the Holy Spirit may teach us (decrypt or decode for us) all things until we become conformed to God's likeness, **WORD**. Accordingly, we may be in the **WORD** (in that we are clothed in the righteousness of God) and the **WORD** in us (God lives in us, for we are the temple of his Holy Spirit). We hence become as one with Jesus and the FATHER dwelling all together, as **WORD**. In view of that, Jesus said, *"On that day you will realize that I am in my Father, and you are in me, and I am in you. (*John 14:20*NIV)*. As we increasingly take on the nature of the **WORD** we increasingly are enabled to do the works that Jesus did and even greater works.

This is something one will not know just based on the fact that Jesus is resurrected and has gone to be with His

Father. One will know because of the effect the resurrection has on one's life. Jesus in commenting that when resurrected He would go to the Father and would ask the Father to send another comforter, who would live in us and dwell with us always. He was pointing out that when the Holy Spirit comes and lives in us and begins to teach us things and function through our lives, then will we be able to appreciate the concept of Christ living in us and we being in him. John's report of the conversation of Jesus with his disciples depicts this:

[7] If you really knew me, you would know my Father as well. From now on, you do know him and have seen him." [8] Philip said, "Lord, show us the Father and that will be enough for us." [9] Jesus answered: "Don't you know me, Philip, even after I have been among you such a long time? Anyone who has seen me has seen the Father. How can you say, 'Show us the Father'? [10] Don't you believe that I am in the Father, and that the Father is in me? The words I say to you are not just my own. Rather, it is the Father, living in me, who is doing his work. [11] Believe me when I say that I am in the Father and the Father is in me; or at least believe on the evidence of the miracles themselves. [12] I tell you the truth, anyone who has faith in me will do what I have been doing. He will do even greater things than these, because I am going to the Father. [13] And I will do whatever you ask in my name, so that the Son may bring glory to the Father. [14] You may ask me for anything in my name, and I will do it. [15] "If you love me, you will obey what I command. [16] And I will ask the Father, and he will give you another Counselor to be with you forever -[17] the Spirit of

*truth. **The world cannot accept him, because it neither sees him nor knows him.** But you know him, for he lives with you and will be in you.* (John 14:7-17 NIV)

Hallelujah!

*[21]Whoever has my commands and obeys them, he is the one who loves me. He who loves me will be loved by my Father, and I too will love him and show myself to him."[22] Then Judas (not Judas Iscariot) said, **"But, Lord, why do you intend to show yourself to us and not to the world?"** [23]Jesus replied, **"If anyone loves me, he will obey my teaching. My Father will love him, and we will come to him and make our home with him.** [24] He who does not love me will not obey my teaching. These words you hear are not my own; they belong to the Father who sent me.* (John 14:21-24 NIV)

Such a mind blowing realization even the disciples had difficulty grasping. No one can understand such things unless the Holy Spirit reveals it; and the Holy Spirit had not yet come to dwell in the disciples. It is no surprise then if the world cannot understand the things of God. A person will not understand if the love of God is not in them. The love of the **WORD** must be in you. It is the **WORD - HOLY SPIRIT that abides with you that will decode or reveal the encrypted mysteries of God to you.** (Related references)[8]

---

[8] *Behold, thou desirest truth in the inward parts: and in the hidden part thou shalt make me to know wisdom* (Ps 51:6).

Word Perfect

A Perfect Man

Encryption is only engaged where communicating parties consider the matter of their discourse private, sensitive and valuable. The conversation will only involve selected parties invested in the relationship. God provides us with encrypted messages devoted to guide us onto a course of redemption. His mission is to reconcile or make perfect again those elected to be eternally his.

God has always invested in relationships. We saw this displayed in his relationship with Adam. When God created Adam, He went further to set aside some time on a daily basis to relate with Adam. We read in the Bible about how God walked and talked with Adam in the garden. A similar relationship existed with Moses, Noah, Abraham and others. God not only set aside time to meet with these men so that He could give them instructions but He spent time in communion with them. Whenever there is a problem in a relationship with God He has always provided

---

*But whoso keepeth his word, in him verily is the love of God perfected: hereby know we that we are in him (*1 John 2:5*).*

*And I will give thee the treasures of darkness, and hidden riches of secret places, that thou mayest know that I, the Lord, which call thee by thy name, am the God of Israel (*Isa 45:3*).*

man a way whereby the fellowship can be restored. In those instances God always looks for a man who He can use to bridge the gap and restore the relationship to the standard He desires. No matter how angry God gets He looks for a man to represent the party of grievance, to ensure an opportunity for redemption, before he chastises or destroys any person or people. He is a just God.

We may not understand how God chooses who He does but He always looks for someone who bears the criteria for redemption. We know that God's criteria are different from ours because man looks at the outward appearance of a person but God looks at the heart *(1Sam 16:7).*

The approach God employed when Adam fell is therefore very understandable, God in this situation also sought to reconnect with Adam. He desired to restore the relationship he had where God and man could communicate heart to heart. Someone was needed to foster the reconciliation of God and man. This person had to represent what God created. He needed to be in God's own image after His own similitude and with his own nature.

The one to be chosen had to possess what Adam now lacked in his nature; he must have all God bears in his nature.

Adam's nature had become infected by sin and as a consequence all his offspring would inherit a sinful nature. There was no pure remnant of God's creation on the earth, and this meant no one was found fit to serve the purpose of redemption. All had sinned and fallen short of God's glory, his expectation. Everyone was now lacking as a being from which God could derive pleasure, because the sinful nature cannot please God.

God's solution therefore was to send his only begotten son, to be born in flesh and be slain as the sacrificial lamb for the redemption of man.

Jesus therefore, came at his father's request; he took on imperfection and became clothed in sin as man was, but still bearing the pure nature, the pure bloodline of God, with the object of reconciling imperfection to perfection.

Hebrews 10:14 states:
Because by one sacrifice he has made perfect forever those who are being made holy (NIV).

Another translation reads:

For by one offering he hath perfected for ever them that are sanctified (KJV).

This gesture would pave the way for the erasure of man's sin and reconcile man to the perfect nature of God. For this to take effect, each person must choose to be reconciled or not. To choose to reconcile a person must believe in his heart that Jesus died for his sins and confess with his mouth that God raised him from the dead. This is how we receive the gift of salvation which restores us to God and allow us to be like Jesus, the Word and Perfect.

It is often asked however, can there ever be a "perfect man"?

The Standard for Eternal Life

The goal of a Christian is to be like Christ. The purpose of the Christian, as for every person, is to bring pleasure to God. A home and all the things of which it consist, is for the owner's pleasure. Each item in the home however brings pleasure in its own unique way to make the home what the owner desires.

> **A person's purpose in life is the unique role God has assigned that person in the overall context of mankind bringing him pleasure.**

If we each have our own purpose, why then does anyone care or need to live their life trying to be like Jesus Christ? God requires that we all do if we choose to remain his children. Being like Jesus is also being like God as they are both one, this is the evidence that we are restored to God's nature. We need to be a spiritual **clone** of Christ but each carrying out our own function. We operate by the same rules even though our purpose in the kingdom is different.

Man cannot please God when he functions from a sinful nature and so a standard must be met.

A standard is a level of quality or attainment. There are various types of standards; among them is the ideal standard. An ideal standard is one that represents optimality, that which is achieved if all things are perfect and operating perfectly. In business the ideal standard is usually seen as unachievable. God's ideal standard however, must be attained.

> **Christ is the ideal standard required by God, everyone must meet this standard as a prerequisite for eternal life.**

God knowing that man on his own cannot achieve the requirement to be reunited in complete fellowship with him, made provision for that lack. God has provided salvation and as such enables perfection (**the state where nothing is lacking**) to be achieved.

Whenever the word "perfect" was used in the Bible in the context of being complete in every regard, needing nothing, finished, it was to bring to bear the standard God requires of the believer to obtain eternal life **or** to show benefits of functioning from that standard.

> **God's standard of being "perfect", where nothing is lacking, has been attained only by Jesus Christ and is only attainable by the believer, through Jesus Christ.**

We therefore see various references to this desired standard:

"Be ye therefore perfect, even as your Father which is in heaven is perfect". Mat 5:48

"And be not conformed to this world: but be ye transformed by the renewing of your mind, that ye may prove what is that good, and acceptable, and perfect, will of God". Rom 12:2

"But when that which is perfect is come, then that which is in part shall be done away". 1Cor 13:10

*"Till we all come in the unity of the faith, and of the knowledge of the Son of God, **unto a perfect man, unto the measure of the stature of the fullness of Christ"*** Eph 4:13

These scriptures communicate "Perfect" as our ideal state of being, what we must look like when we are complete and achieve God's ideal standard. All attribute to that state where we are like God complete wanting nothing for him to say to us at the judgment, enter my good and faithful servant. This is not easily achievable by man, because man has inherited a sinful nature. This nature is at odds with what God really requires of man's conduct. So who can accomplish this feat? The disciples themselves asked this question of Jesus: "...who then can be saved?" Mat 19:25 In other words, who can be perfect? Who will ever qualify to have eternal life? Nobody can achieve what you are asking Jesus. To which Jesus responded: "...with men this is impossible; but with God all things are possible" (Matt 19:26)[9]. On our own we cannot achieve perfection, that state where we are like Christ, but we can with God's help. He has provided a means whereby we who believe can have everlasting life:

> *For God so loved the world that he gave his son so that whoever believes shall have eternal life.* John 3:16

Every person has an area in their life which is the main thorn, that strategic area which the devil uses to taunt and haunt them. Past hurt, failure, an area of your life the effects of which like pain, manifest itself throughout the whole spiritual body. The "Spiritual Achilles Heel" which similar to a multiple symptomatic disease, does not manifest in one area but as problems in several areas of the spiritual life. To cure it one must be keen to identify the root and diligent to persevere through whatever suffering to bring the flesh under subjection. Finding the strength to overcome such lack, frees us to function at our best. This was the effort that utterly frustrated Paul, when he seemingly screamed, oh wretched man that I am, what shall save me from the body of this death? When I try to do good evil presents itself..... (Rom 7:24)

---

[9] I can do all things through Christ who strengthens me (Philippians 4:13).

This is the pivotal nature of sin in our being observed by James when he wrote:

> *"For in many things we offend all. If any man offend not in word, the same is a perfect man, and able also to bridle the whole body".* James 3:2

> *And the tongue is a fire, a world of iniquity: so is the tongue among our members, that it defileth the whole body, and setteth on fire the course of nature; and it is set on fire of hell.* James 3:6

One may wonder why God persists with man when we have become so flawed. What would cause God the perfect all-knowing one to choose someone like Moses to lead his people? Did God forget Moses was a murderer? Why would God declare David a man after his own heart? God knew David would commit ghastly acts before he made the declaration but He said it anyway. Why? If you were in God's circle at that moment what would you think? Would your counsel to God be something like?

> *Ah, my Lord, why would you say such a thing? God, of all the persons to say that is a man after your own heart - David? I know you have been God through the ages, have you begun to become senile? David who wants a woman so bad, he kills her husband in order that he could have her to himself; remember Lord? You should retract that statement right away. We must let everyone know you made a mistake, this was lapsus linguae, a slip of the*

tongue. Lord we must let everyone know that you miss-spoke. Surely Lord you cannot equate David to yourself in this manner. God! Why would you say such a thing?

Would your thoughts be something like that? Ummh. Is it possible that God sees an area of vulnerability not only an indication of a point of weakness, but its association with great strength or potential? A King of a country is its highest authority and power, but an enemy knows if the king can be subdued, the kingdom will be in quandary. The King's office therefore is not only a symbol of power but also of strategic vulnerability. Does that imply that a kingdom is better off without a King? The rise to great heights in any sense often comes with great thrills and benefits; it invariably also bears the risks of great pain and suffering should the tables turn.

The irony is that our motives determine how we focus and our focus determines our outcome. If the enemy is attacking you in an area, what does God want to do with that gift or ability you have which the enemy thinks must be undermined?

People may focus on your weakness; God is aware of your latent strengths, the potential. To borrow a proverbial phrase, God knows, *"don't throw out the baby with the bath water"*. Maybe this is why it is so important to God how we respond to sin. A great warrior cannot only be great when he is standing in the fight, he must also be strong to fight back and stand, after he is knocked down in the fight.

We all are in a battle against the fleshly nature, how we rise when we fall, our display of grit and mettle to persevere and continually advance is the most profound statement of our position of heart; and God looks at the heart.

Where does your strength lie? Often a person involved in embezzlement is one who is good with money and earning trust. We do not fail spiritually simple because we are poor in an area, we fail sometimes because we are very good and the devil desires to destroy this area of strength so that God cannot use it. **Whatever God wants to use in you for good, the devil will seek to influence for a reciprocal purpose.**

We should re-evaluate the areas of our life we consider "weak". For what could God use my ability in such "weak" areas? God is the giver of all good gifts. Therefore every gift, talent or ability we have was given by God and meant for good and for his pleasure. The devil has not given anyone a gift or ability. The devil comes in our lives to steal, to kill and to destroy. He seeks to influence our use of what we already have, for evil purposes. When we allow the devil's influence to take root that's when it manifest itself as a weakness because we have not been strong to choose in that moment, to rely on God and stand against the devices of the enemy. What it really boils down to, is that we are giving the devil control over areas of our life where God needs to be given control.

The fact is someone is always in control of your assets. Whatever you have been given by God is your asset, you decide who controls that, either the devil will or God will. You decide who gets control but you do not get to keep control. Your assets function under one or the other's influence, God or mammon.

When we give the devil control of our assets, the more he uses them, the more and more they become "ab-used". When we give God control of our assets, the more he uses them, the more and more they become "use-full".

The Requirement

In the New Testament Bible, it is interesting to note the manner in which **"perfect"** is used with relation to the **"perfect"** man and that with which **"perfect"** is used in relation to the lamb for the purpose of sacrifice. In relation to the **"perfect"** man, **"perfect"** refers to one who is complete, as in mature or fully developed. While in relation to a sacrificial lamb **"perfect"** is used to communicate, without spot or blemish, without defect.

Jesus the standard to which the believer must be reconciled was chosen as the **perfect** Lamb of God and was offered up as a sacrifice for the sins of man. Christ in this role had to be **perfect**, without spot or blemish in character or trait, untarnished.

For the believer, **perfect** is mature. To be mature spiritually we must reach that final or desired state God requires of us as individuals.

> **Maturity does not suggest that we do not err in our conduct. It suggests however, that we have undergone development that allows us to employ stable, appropriate consideration and judgment in our conduct, including how we respond to our errors. Maturity suggests we err less, and when we do make mistakes, there is more often than not, an immediate, instinctive approach to correct action.**

There is therefore the spiritual state of perfection, where:

a) **We become WORD, like the Father needing nothing to be complete and functioning as the Father and Christ does, as one.**

b) **The lesser state where one is perfect in maturity, achieving that of which God knows we are capable when we are at our best.**

> **The deficit between the two states is provided for by God's grace. Jesus Christ by his blood**

reconciles us to himself. He is the propitiation for our sins. (1Jn 2:2, 1Jn 4:10) Therefore, after our best effort, where we fall short of "Perfect", he has already provided so that we will find favour with the Father. Our best self is not defined by us but is known by God.

God knows our capacity and has designated the purpose of our lives based on our individual, optimal capability. To achieve our best self is to achieve the purpose for which God has us here. We can fulfil our purpose if we follow God's guidance for our daily living and make each decision with his help. We must commit to every task with total conviction and zeal and also ensure that the glory for every success we achieve is attributed to Him.

We all have the ability to fulfil our God given purpose because our purpose was not simply designated to us; we were designed for our purpose.

It would be the exception for a potter to design a vessel and then decide for what it is made. Invariably the potter identifies a purpose and creates a vessel for that purpose.

God knows every person from the beginning. He knows the talents and abilities He has invested in each of us and of what each is capable. Every person is responsible for their best effort towards the goal of God's higher calling. The person who is given one talent will be judged against his capacity in that regard, as will he that has five talents, and so on.

God takes care of the deficit beyond your human capability; you are responsible for your best effort.

Is it not interesting how life unfolds sometimes? Have you ever had a job at which you excelled? You did so well that one day you were given a promotion. Having taken on the new job you find it's different. It's different because, whereas you know some things, you also realize there is a level of inadequacy which you have and you must learn some more in order that you can perform competently at this new level. **Growth always stretches one and takes one into new and unfamiliar territory.** As we grow it becomes necessary to deal with unfamiliar feelings and demands of one nature or other, we go through growing pains. In such circumstances it's not uncommon that one might require help to survive.

I believe the Christian walk is similar, in that, we at times feel comfortable where we are as a Christian and we can go about our lives on cruise control it seems. We are among people with whom we are comfortable; they have accepted us for who we are. We have become comfortable with navigating our lives in familiar spiritual territory. We have become complacent, so much that the devil really doesn't even bother us too much anymore, he too has realized we are just "marking time" with much activity but no advancement. Then comes the time when God steps things up a notch and we find that we do not feel so saved anymore. We question our lives because now we find ourselves exhibiting behaviours and tendencies that are foreign to us. Sometimes inherent traits not yet dealt with now surface. We now begin to ask ourselves, whose life is this? Is it not strange how a preliminary wash of the white linen can show up the real stubborn stains which seem less distinct before it was washed at all? It should be cleaner, but now we are not so sure this thing can be used anymore, this is an ugly stain; I never saw this before. Now we have to pull out the harsh stain remover, just soap and water will not work. The sheet requires the right handling if it must be preserved, otherwise the fabric could be destroyed. **What with right handling could be maintained as a piece of pride, may have to be thrown out as garbage if not attended to competently.**

Whereas the blood of Jesus cleanses us from all sins, as God brings us into higher levels of spiritual growth we find that latent aspects of our sinful nature comes to fore. People look on and may see signs of things we need to deal with, but what they may not understand is that we are seeing these things sometimes for the first time as well. They judge, forgetting that this path of growth requires that God is constantly uprooting things of the sinful nature to bring us into the manifestation of our best self. Even though others may not have the same issue, everyone has their own stains that must be cleaned.

Nothing should stop us from being laundered by Christ as only he is able to keep us from falling. Our aim must be as his, that we be presented faultless before the presence of his glory with exceeding great joy. (Jude verse 24)

While we strive to be like Christ we will never be totally like Christ through our own efforts. It is he who will enable us to be transformed into his likeness. As we aspire and make sincere efforts, he will allow us to evolve and become the best that we can be. In this state of commitment Christ presents us to His father and he clothed us in his righteousness as a gesture of grace, so that when the father sees us, he no longer sees our inadequacy or any lack but sees a reconciled man, presented to him in perfection. He looks on us and He sees Jesus, the Word, and He sees himself. In this state God will give to every man the things which he has covenanted according to his riches in Christ Jesus; He will give us eternal life. As stated in *Rom 2:6-7*

> *⁶ who will judge each person according to their deeds and discharge the negative impact reflected on record because of those actions: ⁷ to those who steadfastly persevered to do what is excellent and honourable, and pursued the incorruptible prize; He compensates them with eternal life.*

The Responsibility

What then, is our responsibility since we believe? Can we do as we please all because we know that God has already provided for our salvation? Of course not! We have obligations.

The ability with which God has enriched our lives is for our self-actualization but within the greater context of our servant hood. We will be our best when we serve God within the parameters of his design. It is a role with obligation to self, to others and to God.

Ephesians 4 states:

*[10] He that descended is the same also that ascended up far above all heavens, **that he might fill (as in, add all that is necessary to make complete, lacking nothing for full measure, make perfect) all things.***

*[11] And he gave some, apostles; and some, prophets; and some, evangelists; and some, pastors and teachers; [12] **For the perfecting of the saints, for the work of the ministry, for the edifying of the body of Christ:***

*[13] Till we all come in the unity of the faith, and of the knowledge of the Son of God, unto a perfect man, **unto the measure of the stature of the fulness of Christ ....[15] But speaking the truth in love, may grow up into him in all things, which is the head,***

even Christ: (to spiritually mature into all things which are characteristic of Christ) Eph 4:10-15.

Christ has provided through the various gifts of the body of Christ all that is necessary for us to grow and mature into his likeness. Where we fail to achieve through that provision he extends more grace. As long as we are sincere in our efforts to reach the mark, he continues to extend grace. If we have the commitment he has the grace, and each time we fall he will help us back to our feet and when our feet are too weak to go any further he will carry us that are committed.

To attain Perfection (the fullness of Christ, where the believer is lacking nothing and can enter into eternal life), the believer's life will therefore involve the following factors:

- The investment of believers with variable gifts to help nourish and amplify another's own gifts.
- The development of one's own life by enrichment of one's innate abilities, through the earnest desire and pursuit of spiritual gifts. The selfless utilization of gifts and abilities for the wellbeing of individuals in the body of Christ and ultimately the body at large. This is what each believer must bring to the table, be all that you can be , your full potential in talents and abilities in Christ and make your contribution towards the development of others.

- God's provision of grace through the blood of Christ. This is the Contribution Christ has made through his blood to bridge the gap that we through our best efforts will never have attained in order to be perfect for eternal life.

The believer has a responsibility of stewardship. Stewardship for the gifts and talents God has given him, for the investment of others in him and for his own abilities and his responsibility to invest in others. We are our brother's keeper.

We have obligations:

- We have an obligation to ourselves. - God has equipped us with every resource that we need to be our best. **That which comes from inside a vessel is no purer than the vessel itself** (*so first clean the inside of the vessel.... Matt 23:26*). **Our state affects everything we are involved in or come in contact with.** Our obligation to glorify God and to up lift our brethren is affected by our state of being, by that which is happening in our life. We have a responsibility first to ensure our own happiness and well-being and to secure our eternal destiny before anything or anyone else. When we ride aboard an airplane, security advisory lets us know first put your oxygen mask on, then assist your child or anyone else.

Our effectiveness to assist someone else is weakened the more we are at risk. While we may never be in a perfect situation to help, we are more effective if our position or wellbeing is stable or reinforced. Our greatest obligation in life is to secure our own eternal destiny. *(See Matt 25: 1-13)*

Paul's encouragement reminded Timothy that scriptures are inspired by God and available for the beneficial purposes as a doctrinal guide, for conviction and correction in our daily lives. (2Tim 3:16-17) The Bible is the manual that instructs how to walk accurately before God. We should use God's word to guide us into developing each unique gift that God has given us so that we can maximize our potential in every endeavour. This we do as outlined in 2Cor 7:1

"... cleanse ourselves from all filthiness of the flesh and spirit, perfecting holiness in the fear of God."

We are encouraged to exercise great will and persevere to accomplish excellence operating in our God given gifts (2Cor 8:11). We must pursue this, understanding that God has invested in us.

¹²I do not want you to think that I consider myself as one who has achieved complete perfection. I follow Christ with zeal to grasp the things of the kingdom, a calling to which Christ has persuaded me and I am committed. ¹³Brethren, as much as I do not yet fully comprehend all that pertains to it, this one thing I do know, I have put the past behind me and I am fully engaged to achieve the goal ahead. ¹⁴With the help of Christ I will persevere to achieve the level of excellence God requires of me. Phil 3:12-14

¹⁵⁻¹⁶Let us be united to this same end, even if you think that you have already arrived and are perfect lacking in nothing, let us follow the same doctrine and pursue the same goal. God will reveal to us if we should be otherwise concerned. Phil 3:15-16

As James instructs:

> *Perseverance must finish its work so that you may be mature and complete, not lacking anything. James 1:4 NIV*

Paul also reminds us:

> *⁹For we have a measure of knowledge and we prophesy with a measure of knowledge the Holy Spirit imparts. ¹⁰But when that which is perfect, complete in entirety, is come, then that which is partial will end. ¹² For now we see a blurred reflection; but then face to face: now I know in a given measure; but then shall I become thoroughly acquainted with him, knowing how he would act in every situation, just as he knows everything about me. 1Cor 13:9-10, 12*

- We have an obligation to God - God wants a return on his investment. If an investor is pleased, you know that he is satisfied with the return on his investment. God must be pleased with our life. We please him by the way we acknowledge him, serve him, serve others, use our gifts to honour him and in general, conduct our lives in a way that brings value to his name. *(See Matt 25: 14-30)*

Christ was sent into the world by his father and he has now sent the believer into the world ("*Go ye into all the world...."Mk 16:15*). In the world Christ did as he saw his father do and requires us to do as we saw him Christ, do. He has prayed for us that our faith will not fail, that our joy may be full, also that all may be one; as he and the Father are one. Christ in us, and God in Christ, so that we may be made perfect in one *(John 17:18-26)*. Here we bring God pleasure by fulfilling his desire for the restoration of our fellowship with him and his son.

- We have an obligation to the brethren - The Apostle Paul was exemplary in his relationship with Timothy by displaying our role in supporting each other towards the goal of becoming our best self. In his letter to Timothy he reminded him of how he put hands on him for the stirring up of the gifts of God in him. (2Tim 1:6). Peter also showed the same dutifulness to encouraging the brethren (2Peter 1:13, 2Peter 3:1). It is human that at times we let our guard down, we become lax and may even lose zeal and focus of our calling. It is in times like these that in our best interest we are in love nudged by one in the body of Christ, to urge us onto good works. *(See Matt 25: 31-46)*

God will judge how we fulfil the aforementioned obligations.

Judgment may not be about what we could not do. Judgment may be about how we did the things that we have the capacity to do or whether we choose to do those things at all. The Judgment

of God may in essence be an evaluation of how we exercised our own judgement.

Reconciled

Reconciliation becomes necessary:

- Where state of affairs disagree in circumstances where they are meant to be the same.

- When accounts are required to agree but at the time of presentation a variance exist.

- Where parties are at odds.

Reconciliation is the process whereby a difference or cause of conflict is identified and a means is reached to end the disparity. It is a strategy that accounts for differences and brings accounts or parties into agreement.

Sin generated a variance between God and man whom He created. Though created children of light, Adam's unwise choice corrupted him and caused his whole lineage to become children of darkness, children possessing a sinful nature. **Mankind became a creature with a natural or default tendency to sin.** Man's nature became so tainted that everything he did was affected by sin. Consequently, everything man did, every decision, every action is now done with a natural propensity to contrive evil. If this seems dark, that's because it is. The Bible states:

*"...God saw that the wickedness of man was great in the earth, and that **every imagination of the thoughts of his heart was <u>only evil continually</u>"**.* Gen 6:5(see also: psm14:3, Rom 1:29-31, Rom 39:19)

The reasoning of man is deceitful and utterly corrupted (Jer. 17:9). Man's best efforts to be pure still leave stains of the sinful ways, impurities still linger after all human purgative efforts. Man's best efforts would help him mature but would never make him pure as he was in the beginning. All had sinned and become lacking, short of the glory of God, deficient for the purpose of God's pleasure.

So that no matter what our efforts, if we say we have no sin we deceive ourselves. [10] (1Jn 1:8).

Sadly, it therefore means also, that even when we become mature believers we still have sin. We have become persons who have grown spiritually but still possess a sinful nature, so we still battle with carnal things. Sin is an action or thought which disobeys God's law, a wrong or an offence against Him. We continually perpetrate acts or thoughts which are immoral, unjust or improper in God's eyes. The variance between God and man is sin. When people are in trouble be it a nation, tribe or mankind as a whole God's love propels him to find a way to save them. In those circumstances God always looks for a man to represent the cause for the salvation of that people. In one instance Noah was chosen to stand in the gap, where God was on the brink of destroying all creatures, mankind and

---

[10] *And moreover I saw under the sun the place of judgment, that wickedness was there; and the place of righteousness, that iniquity was there.* Eccl 3:16

animals, the whole lot, *"But Noah found grace[11] in the eyes of the Lord"*. *Gen 6:8*

In the case of Sodom and Gomorrah they were destroyed because none righteous could be found in the land.

Ezekiel 22:30 (NIV) states:

*"I looked for someone among them who would build up the wall and stand before me in the gap on behalf of the land **so I would not have to destroy it**, but I found no one".*

The need arose and the question was also posed, in the matter concerning humanity as a whole, who would stand in the gap for the salvation of the world? In this matter of eternal life, God also found no one worthy to be the reconciliatory factor. He had tried before, having a high priest that would represent the people and make sacrifices for the remission of their sins. The ceremonial approach proved to have a "white-out effect". The error is covered over, a form of erasure, but you can tell every time you go to the page that an error was there and you may even remember the details of the mistake.

The shedding of Blood is necessary for the sacrifice and the cleansing but the blood of animals will not suffice for the remission of the sins of man. No matter how pure the animal it will not completely remove the stain. Animals do not possess the spirit and nature of mankind. God did not breathe into the nostrils of animals; they do not comprise

---

[11] Grace is defined as God's unmerited or undeserved favour.

the spirit and abilities of God which was only imparted to man. Man must be redeemed by pure blood but it must be of a man, a being with the pure nature of God, a pure man.

For the law by Moses whereby a high priest would atone for the sins of the people through a ceremonial routine was an imperfect form of what God would later implement. It was not God's select provision. The sacrifices of animals and the shedding of their blood did not permanently atone for the sins of the people and so atonement needed to be made yearly. For it is not possible that the blood of bulls and of goats should take away sins. Because these sacrifice and offering did not please God, he was not appeased concerning the sins of man. He therefore, prepared a body for his only son so that Christ would come and be the perfect sacrificial lamb to be slain for the sins of mankind. As such, Jesus Christ came to fulfil his father's will. (Heb 9:9-14, Heb 10:1-7)

*And she shall bring forth a son, and thou shalt call his name JESUS: for he shall save **his** people from their sins. Matt 1:21*

Wherefore, as by one man sin entered into the world, and death by sin; and so death passed upon all men, for that all have sinned: Rom 5 :12

[14].....the love of Christ constraineth us; because we thus judge, that if one died for all, then were all dead: [15] And that he died for all, that they which live should not henceforth live unto themselves, but unto him which died for them, and rose again. 2 Cor 5:14-15

The mystery of God's love is embraced in the fact that God loved his only begotten son so much, He considered him the only one worthy enough to appease him for the thing that brought him greatest anguish. He would do anything for his son. **Jesus Christ loves his father so much that he would do anything to help heal the hurt his father felt from the vileness of fallen man.** And **God loves mankind so much that he would do anything to find a way to save man.**

To save mankind God sacrificed his son, the embodiment of his greatest love, to express the depth of his love for mankind. His son submitted to be sacrificed as an expression of the depth of his love for the Father and that he would please him at any cost, and man's response? **What is your response? Now that provision has been made for you to be reconciled to God, what is your response?**

It is not so much that we loved God, but that He loved us and sent His son to save us. If God loves us this much, we should make the effort to love one another. If we love one another, we will be demonstrating God's love and so know that His love is in us. If God's love dwells in us, His love adds what we are lacking in order that we may become complete. As our love is made complete in him, **we are confident that we may have boldness in the Day of Judgment,** *because as he is, so are we in this world. (See Heb 10:19-26)*

Nuggets -The Encrypted Word Received From God

1. Every WORD (intangible) has the potential to become something of substance (tangible).
2. Words have the power to transform.
3. We decide if words impact us.
4. Thoughts come from one of two sources, God or the devil.
5. Words can do, only if I do...
6. Words have power but I have power over words.
7. Words I believe are empowered by what I speak.
8. Man must be born again not so that our form will change but so that our substance, our spirit is changed.
9. Logos is dynamic; it can change its substantive form.
10. The word comes to continuously transform our spirit to be like God, in spirit, mind and power.
11. God's word is encrypted, coded.
12. God wants us to have a relationship with His word as it was in the beginning.
13. God desires we become the WORD, just as Jesus is the WORD, and dwell with Him.
14. Every word spoken by God to us is designed to accomplish a specific "THING".
15. We can only accomplish our purpose, that thing for which God has placed us in this world, when we come into alignment with God's word for our lives.
16. You must take so that you will not break.

17. The Holy Spirit decodes God's word to us, to accomplish a designated thing in our lives and this helps us to grow and be increasingly transformed into God's spiritual image and likeness.
18. Our motives determine how we focus and our focus determines our outcome.
19. Whatever God wants to use in you for good, the devil will seek to influence for a reciprocal purpose.
20. Whatever you have been given by God is your asset. Either the devil or God will control your assets. You decide who gets control but you do not get to keep control.
21. You were designed for your purpose.

GOD'S SWEETNESS, NOT WEAKNESS

A Terrible God

We often see God portrayed as an all-loving, all-powerful, and impartial God. After all, if God is love, how could there be so many catastrophes involving the death of his creation? Sometimes people choose to speak of God in such simplistic manner, sweet and syrupy but tantamount to patronizing Him. They use words that make it seem that we can twirl God around our little finger and have our way with Him; somewhat like a young girl who knows she has her daddy at her fingertips.

No matter how mad he gets with her about something, she can come five minutes later, hug his neck, give him a butterfly kiss on the cheek and take his wallet and car keys. Well who wouldn't want to have a god like that? The only question then would be; who is the one being worshipped?

Our God is most loving, merciful and kind, but **He is also the powerful God of horrendous possibilities.** God is not our cuddly teddy bear. He is to be feared, as in having a profound respect for Him. It must be understood that He is also a terrible God. There is nothing gentle or dainty about the adjective terrible; terrible is one of those adjectives that actually convey a meaning of something or someone being extreme and very unpleasant. Terrible means not nice! Synonymous with awful, dire, dreadful, fearful, fearsome, frightening, horrendous, horrific, atrocious, abominable, painful; get the picture? Not nice, terrible! While at times the word conveys awe-inspiring or wonderful, mostly, the many uses of the word are associated with things being downright dreadful.

Deuteronomy chapter 28 demonstrates this terrible side of God. God made a covenant with Israel. He outlined what He would do if Israel obeyed his commandments and if they failed to do so.

Under this covenant if Israel in obeying God, obeyed all His commandments, they again would see the kind, loving, merciful God, and benefit from his blessings (Deut 28:1-14). Some of the blessings were[12]:

A. [1]He would make Israel the most excellent and powerful nation in all respects, high above all other nations of the earth.
B. [2]These blessings would come to Israel and always be theirs in abundance.

- [3]They would be blessed in whatever business they engaged, whether in the city or in the field.

---

[12] Superscripts in the following sections refer to the corresponding verses of Deuteronomy Chapter 28.

- ⁴The fruit of their bodies, their farms, their cattle, sheep and any other animals they raised would be blessed.
- ⁵Their harvest would be blessed and they would always have abundance in store.
- ⁶Wherever they went, and whatever they did would be blessed.
- ⁷The Lord would cause those who attack Israel to be defeated before their face; their enemies would come against them as a united force, and flee before them in confusion.
- ⁹The Lord would permanently set them as his holy people, just as he swore to them that He would, if they would obey His commandments and walk in all his ways.
- ¹⁰All the people on earth would know that Israel is God's special people; and would give them due respect.
- ¹²The Lord would open to them the heavens, His plenteous storehouse, to give rain to their crops at the right time, and to bless all the work of their hands. They would give loans to many nations, and would not need to borrow.

- [13]The Lord would make them the head, and not the tail; they would be above only and not be beneath; if they obeyed the commandments of the Lord their God, to observe and do them:
- [14]And would not stray from any of the words which God commands, to the right hand, or to the left, or serve other gods.

These are God's awesome promises that he would bring to bear **if Israel obeyed Him and served Him only**. Who would not want to live under such a promise? Know however, that it is a reciprocal relationship as the reciprocity of God is consistent when it comes to covenant. His blessings and His promises come with conditions. God always desires something from a relationship He establishes. He wants glory. He will bless us if we denounce all other gods and serve **HIM ONLY**. If we do not fulfil His commandment, He will pour out His wrath. With each covenant God leaves us to make a decision, a choice; eternal life or eternal death, blessing or curse. We must choose wisely!

If Israel would not obey God, follow all his commands and abide by His law as He instructed, they would see how terrible He could be! Curses would come upon them, pursue them and overtake them until they would all be destroyed (Deut 28:15-68).

- ¹⁶They would be cursed in whatever business they engage, whether in the city or in the field.
- ¹⁷Their harvest would be cursed, their storehouse would always be empty and they would not have enough to eat.
- ¹⁸The fruit of their bodies, their farms, their cattle, sheep and any other animals they raise would be cursed.
- ¹⁹Wherever they went, and whatever they did would be cursed.

- ²⁰The Lord would send upon them curses, aggravation and reprimand, in all that they set their hand to do, until they were quickly destroyed and perished; **because of the wickedness they did and for having forsaken Him**.
- ²¹The Lord would cause them to be afflicted with terrible diseases. The diseases would stay with them until all of them in the Promised Land were dead, totally wiped out.

- ^{22}The Lord would smite them with diseases that progressively waste their tissues, with severe fever and painful swellings. He would blast their crops with fiery scorching winds, drought and fungus. These curses would be on them relentlessly until they perished.
- ^{23}Their sky would be like brass, sealed, they would have no rain and the ground would become hard like iron.
- ^{24}The Lord would make powder and dust come down from the sky like rain onto their land until they are destroyed.

- ^{25}The Lord would cause Israel to be attacked and defeated by their enemies. Israel would go to war against their enemies as a united force, and flee before them in confusion.
- ^{26}Crows and wild animals would eat their dead bodies; no one would be left to drive the scavengers away.

If they did not choose to serve the Lord God with joyfulness and with gladness of heart, punishment was their lot.

- Furthermore the Lord would send against them enemies and would cause them to be the slaves of these enemies, without food, drink or any clothes to wear; in total poverty: until he destroyed them.

- He would bring a country from a great distance to invade their land, a merciless nation that would not have pity on anyone, not even the young or the old. This country would exploit their resources including crops and animals, until everything and everyone is destroyed.

- Israel would be besieged and oppressed to the point where they would begin to eat their own children born to them during the besieged period.

The same loving God, who would have blessed Israel above all other nations if they forsake all gods and worshipped him, now says:

" .... *as the Lord rejoiced over you to do you good, and to multiply you; so the Lord will rejoice over you to destroy you, and to bring you to nought; and ye shall be plucked from off the land whither thou goest to possess it*" (Deut 28:63).

We cannot hinder God's pleasure. We were created for his pleasure and if we choose to follow all his commandments, exalt and worship him only as God; He will get pleasure from blessing us. If we choose not to, He will still gain as much pleasure, only this time, from our destruction; there are conditions and consequences.

David admonished us "*¹ O clap your hands, all ye people; shout unto God with the voice of triumph. ² For the Lord most high is terrible; he is a great King over all the earth"* Ps 47:1-2. He exhorts us further in Ps 66:3; *"Say unto God, How terrible art thou in thy works! through the greatness of thy power shall thine enemies submit themselves unto thee."*

Whether it is His mighty deeds of love or terrible deeds of damnation God carries out His works on a God-sized scale, well beyond our imagination.

This is what sets Him apart as the awesome God. We see this in another instance where He spoke with Moses: *"Behold, I make a covenant: before all thy people I will do marvels, such as have not been done in all the earth, nor in any nation: and all the people among which thou art shall see the work of the Lord: for it is a terrible thing that I will do with thee."* (Ex 34:10).

God's works will always leave us in awe and totally flabbergasted. His work is done on a level designed to cause fear in the heart of man because He desires that we worship Him. He acts to instil a reverential fear and trust that abhors evil.

Hence Solomon in his wisdom wrote: *"I know that, whatsoever God doeth, it shall be forever: nothing can be put to it, nor any thing taken from it: and God doeth it, that men should fear before him"* (Eccl 3:14).

God makes his chosen ones the centre of His attention and requires that we make Him the centre of our attention.

He will not share us with another. Either you serve God or mammon. You cannot serve two masters, you will hate one, and love the other; or hold to one, and despise the other (Matt 6:24). **Only through worship can we court God.** He invites us into his presence and as we enter into His presence with the right attitude and magnify Him in spirit and in truth, we draw near to Him, He draws near to us, and our fellowship is sweet.

If there was any other god who could do greater works than He whom we deem the true and living God, we would know and ascribe worship unto such god. God is not insecure, He knows He is the invincible one, so we see Him challenge the power of man's other gods and put them to the test (1Kings 18:17-40).

He is a jealous GOD; but He is just. What expectations he has in His relationships are made clear right up-front. So with Israel, concerning His covenant, God makes a clear stipulation as to what His expectations are in His instructions to Moses:

> *[12]Be careful, do not make any covenants with the people in the land where you go, this could become a problem for you. [13]Make sure you destroy their altars and their idols. [14]You shall not worship any other god; I am a jealous God (Ex 34:12-14).*

God still exposes us to His terrible streak from time to time; generally referred to as "Acts of God". [13]He shows off by displaying the might of the wind, dramatic displays of lightning and thunder, mystifying displays of whirlwinds and tornadoes. Somtimes in natural disasters: earthquakes, tsunamis, hurricanes and monsoons in many different parts of the world leaving thousands dead. Would a loving God do such a thing? Why?

We do not always know why God does things, He owes us no explanation. He is God. He hands down wrath from one generation to another and shows mercy to another [14](Deut 5:9-10). We do not have the history of his transactions.

Serving God requires that we trust His heart and know that He continues to be just in all His ways.

---

[13] This topic is dealt with extensively in the Book "Acts of God – The God Factor" visit: www.egmenzies.com for information.

[14] *9Thou shalt not bow down thyself unto them, nor serve them: for I the Lord thy God am a jealous God, visiting the iniquity of the fathers upon the children unto the third and fourth generation of them that hate me, 10 And shewing mercy unto thousands of them that love me and keep my commandments (Deut 5:9-10).*

He Has Favourites

So, is this God some kind of maniac of whom we should be afraid? Should we be very afraid? Well some should be, though the ones who you may think should be afraid, often are those who live wantonly without regard or reverence for God or the things of God. Frankly often it seems such people could care less that God even exist, but the hard truth is, everyone has a place in the Almighty's plan.

God is the mighty King in whose presence we dare not enter without an invitation. To go into the inner court of the King without being called could mean death. Hence David proclaims: *"Blessed is the man whom thou choosest, and causest to approach unto thee, that he may dwell in thy courts: we shall be satisfied with the goodness of thy house, even of thy holy temple"* Ps 65:4. Under the Old Testament the high priest is the only one who could enter into the holy of holies, the very presence of God. He needed to go through a ritual before entering and would need to offer up blood for his sins and the sins of the people. Jesus gave his life to abolish the law so that we can come freely and boldly to the throne of grace that we may obtain mercy and find grace to help in time of need (Heb.4:15-16). This is a liberty or freedom of access that has been bought with the blood of Christ and which no one should take for granted.

It is distasteful to be given privilege by someone of high office to share closeness to them; and then show disrespect by becoming familiar in our conduct. God is our friend. He is our Father, the "I am that I am" and above all else, He is Almighty God.

We are privileged to have God on our side and not against us. Israel had God on their side, an advantage that David summed up when he said: *"and what one nation in the earth is like thy people, even like Israel, whom God went to redeem for a people to himself, and to make him a name, and to do for you great things and terrible, for thy land, before thy people, which thou redeemdst to thee from Egypt, from the nations and their gods?"* (2 Sam 7:23).

He chose Israel, way back when this same terrible God summoned Moses to a meeting with Him on top of Mount Sinai. He required that no one else came with Moses. No one else was permitted in that meeting. It was a closed meeting; He had a plan to unfold to Moses. He would make covenant with Israel; they would be His chosen people. So God comes down in a cloud and He begins to move about declaring Himself, God, "The Lord, The Lord God". Declaring the nature of His rule: "merciful and gracious, longsuffering, and abundant in goodness and truth; keeping mercy for thousands, forgiving sin and that will by no means clear the guilty; visiting the iniquity of the fathers upon the children, and upon the children's children, unto the third and to the fourth generation" (Ex 34:6-8).

Moses knew God meant business; he quickly bowed his head toward the earth, and worshipped. God here already plans to drive out before Israel the Amorites, Canaanites, Hittites, Perizzites, Hivites and the Jebusites (Ex 34:11). What does that mean? Was He going to ask them to leave their land so that Israel could occupy it? Would He have them sit down at a bargaining table to work out something amicable? I don't think so! He was declaring war on those nations. He would slaughter them in battle for Israel, and He is simply bringing Moses in on His plan. **Here is what I**

plan to do for Israel (my favourite people); here is what I require of Israel as party to this covenant. Can you see the benefits of being chosen by God? Of being given preference by God? Do you think the Amorites, Canaanites, Hittites, Perizzites, Hivites, or the Jebusite thought; this is a loving, merciful, gracious, longsuffering God of goodness and truth? I don't think so! They would fear Him by choice or designation. God had set the stage for Israel to see His awesome, marvellous work and those other nations were on the wrong side! Israel being the chosen ones, God's favourite, was able to see His goodness.

God chooses whom He will favour. Everyone cannot be your favourite, you must choose.

David tells us: *Blessed is the man whom God chooses (Ps 65:4)*. This is a harsh reality of God, a truth that most people do not want to hear. It is far easier to market a loving God who is all-inclusive. The Bible truth is that He chooses those who will follow and serve him. You can turn Him down, but He gets to choose. Jesus said: *"No man can come to me, except the Father which hath sent me draw him" (John 6:44)*.

Today there is so much effort to refine things to make them more palatable. Sugar has been refined, flour has been refined; they are bleached and all kinds of stuff done to them. By the time they get to the table for your food, your doctor says "don't eat it, it will kill you!" Sometimes a thing is best in its raw state, its true state. No polishing down or dressing up; just given as is. You cannot improve on God! We sometimes become so wise in our own eyes that we think God's word has to be refined and refined, so it becomes palatable. By the time we finish putting in our synonyms, and homonyms, the **WORD** people get is tantamount to an antonym, a paraphrase, a tall-tale that bears no life-changing power. Paul the Apostle was concerned about this trait he saw forming in the early church. He wrote to the Corinthian church:

"[12] ....we have received, not the spirit of the world, but the spirit which is of God; that we might know the things that are freely given to us of God.[13] Which things also we speak, not in the words which man's wisdom teacheth, but which the Holy Ghost teacheth; comparing spiritual things with spiritual. [14] But the natural man receiveth not the things of the Spirit of God: for they are foolishness unto him: neither can he know them, because they are spiritually discerned." 1Cor 2:12-14

To recap: **God chose Israel and being chosen comes with privileges and responsibilities.**

God's promise to Israel is that if Israel obeys His voice and keeps His covenant, then Israel shall be a peculiar treasure unto Him above all people (Ex 19:5). Israel broke the covenant making it void. God therefore cancelled that covenant. He would now make a new covenant, a better covenant established upon better promises. [15] This new covenant with the house of Israel and the house of Judah would be one of grace not of the law. God would put his law into the people's mind, their intellect and moral understanding. He would put His law on their heart, the centre of man's core nature and He would be their God

---

[15] Jeremiah 31:31-37, Heb 8:8-13

and they would be His people. Each person would be taught not by a scribe but by God. Under the new covenant God said: *"...I will be merciful to their unrighteousness, and their sins and their iniquities will I remember no more."* (Heb 8:12).

The ceremonies under the old covenant would also be put away. Christ (the Messiah) would come as a High Priest of a greater order. He through a greater, more perfect tabernacle not made with human hands and by virtue of His eternal Spirit, offered Himself as an unblemished sacrifice to God. He went once for all into the Holy of Holies of Heaven and by his own blood obtained absolute eternal redemption for all. His sacrifice purged our consciences from dead works to serve the true and living God. Christ having entered into heaven itself, now appears in the presence of God on our behalf. Since the priesthood is now changed; the obligations under the law is abolished (Heb 7:12-13). Christ is therefore able to save to the uttermost whoever comes to God through Him because He lives forever perpetually interceding for the believers (Heb 7: 25-26 KJV, NIV). Thus Christ made salvation available to all people, whether they are Jews or Gentiles. Each person must believe on the Lord Jesus Christ in order to be saved (Acts 15:1-18). This means **salvation is activated when we believe in our heart that Jesus died and was raised from the dead and confess with our mouth the Lord Jesus (Rom 10:9). This new covenant embraces all people who believe on the Lord Jesus Christ. These are the ones who will inherit the promise of the new covenant.**

Even with the advent of grace, the Jews did not all believe Jesus to be the Messiah nor did they obey his gospel. They refused the messiah who was sent to redeem them under the New Testament covenant. The Bible states that He came unto his own (things, creation, home, Jewish people, world,) and his own Jewish people, the chosen people to whom he was first sent, did not welcome (receive or believe) him (John 1:11).

However,

"12...as many as received him, to them gave he power to become the sons of God, even to them that believe on his name: 13 Which were born, not of blood, nor of the will of the flesh, nor of the will of man, but of God. 14 And the Word was made flesh, and dwelt among us, (and we beheld his glory, the glory as of the only begotten of the Father) full of grace and truth. 15 John bare witness of him, and cried, saying, This was he of whom I spake, He that cometh after me is preferred before me: for he was before me. 16 And of his fulness have all we received, and grace for grace. 17 For the law was given by Moses, but grace and truth came by Jesus Christ." John 1:12-17.

However, of the Jews there is a remnant according to the election of grace (Rom 11:5), who answered when the Lord called, when He spoke they listened and did not do evil in His sight but chose to do the things in which God delighted.

The remnant of Israel who believes in Christ as well as the non-Jews (or Gentiles as they are called) who believe and profess faith in Jesus Christ, have now become the spiritual Israel.

For not all those out of Israel (the literal Jewish nation), are of Israel (the spiritual Israel) (Romans 9:6). God also promised Abraham that "in thee shall all nations be blessed" and therefore the heathen justified through faith have become children of Abraham (Gal 3:7-9). We understand therefore that the spiritual Israel is the children of promise. They inherit the privileges under the new covenant and are beneficiaries to the hidden wisdom of God (2 Peter 3:9).

Of importance also is the fact that if God has called a people unto himself and made a covenant with them, there are things available to that group and not to everyone.

The question therefore is; are all privy to becoming a part of the children of promise (the elect). Who are elected to be recipients of the encrypted word and what happens to those who are not a part of the elect?

For Your Eyes and Ears Only

We have seen God establish from the outset that He will favour whom He chooses. Therefore the Bible speaks of the called, according to His purpose. The elect as such has access to God's promise and **the rest** are blinded (or hardened). Paul explained this in his letter to the Romans chapter 11:[16]

"[1] I ask then: Did God reject his people? By no means! I am an Israelite myself, a descendant of Abraham, from the tribe of Benjamin. [2] God did not reject his people, whom he foreknew. Don't you know what the Scripture says in the passage about Elijah — how he appealed to God against Israel: [3] "Lord, they have killed your prophets and torn down your altars; I am the only one left, and they are trying to kill me"? [4] And what was God's answer to him? "I have reserved for myself seven thousand who have not bowed the knee to Baal." [5] So too, at the present time there is a remnant chosen by grace. [6] And if by grace, then it is no longer by works; if it were, grace would no longer be grace. [7]What then? What Israel sought so earnestly it did not obtain, but the elect did. The others were hardened, [8] as it is written:"God gave them a spirit of stupor, eyes so that they could not see and ears so that they could not hear, to this very day." (Rom 11:1-8 NIV).

Jesus explained this to His disciples further in Mark 4:11-12, saying,

*"[11] ... Unto you it is given to know the mystery of the kingdom of God: **but unto them that are without**, all these things are done in parables: [12]That seeing they may see, and not perceive; and hearing they may hear, and not understand; **lest at any time they should be converted, and their sins should be forgiven them**".*

---

[16] References: 1Kings 19:10, 14 and 18. See also: Isa 6:9-10, Matt 13:11, 14-15 & John 12:40

Back in the day, some religious groups had various secrets and signs known only to the initiated members. Jesus did not subscribe to secret signs, but his method of secret revelation to the disciples was through the parables he told. Jesus used the parables to unfold to them the secrets of the kingdom of heaven. The disciples were privy to the secrets of the kingdom because of their relationship with Jesus; they had been initiated into the kingdom. The religious sect of the Pharisees had knowledge of their own signs and secrets, but they were not knowledgeable in the mysteries of the kingdom; from them the secrets were hidden.

Like the disciples, those of us under the covenant of grace, because of our belief in Jesus Christ, we have been saved and have been initiated as God's elect. By the same token, those who have not believed in their heart that Jesus is the son of God, that He died and rose again, are not saved and are therefore not initiated as God's elect. Consequently they have no access to the mysteries of God, they are the ones without (or not elected for the revelation of the mysteries of God), as mentioned in Mark 4:11. Understand also that Jesus spoke in parables so that "seeing they see not and hearing they hear not, neither do they understand". So the unbeliever and the redeemed may see and hear the same thing, but to one it is revelation and truth, and to the other, it is all noise; it is **ENCRYPTED!** So do not be surprised if you read the word of God and receive life giving revelation while some do but cannot make sense of it.

The revelation of the word comes based on a condition of heart. The spiritual eyes are opened

and the spiritual ears hear and one becomes able to discern the things of God when one has a heart of belief.

"But the natural man receiveth not the things of the Spirit of God: for they are foolishness unto him: neither can he know them, because they are spiritually discerned". 1 Cor 2:14

Jesus was saying in effect, I speak to you in parables so that they cannot know our business. *"That it might be fulfilled which was spoken by the prophet, saying, I will open my mouth in parables; I will utter things which have been kept secret from the foundation of the world"* (Matt 13:35). Have you ever been around people who are multilingual? What do they do if they are conversing with friends and want to keep their conversation between themselves? They suddenly switch to a language they believe is unlikely understood by others around. So others hear them speak but do not understand the conversation. So when God speaks to us through His word, whether we are reading or hearing, the word is **ENCRYPTED**. It is meant for only those who have been initiated through their belief in Jesus Christ. Others will not understand and only those, whose spirit through believing in God has been connected or initiated, will be able to understand. They can understand because the Holy Spirit decodes and conveys that which God wishes to communicate. Understand further, a greater dimension to this encryption exist. In Matt 13:11 and Luke 8:10 when Jesus said "unto you it is given to know the mysteries of the kingdom of God: but to **the rest** in parables; that seeing they may not see, and hearing they may not understand"; **"the rest" here also refers to those precluded in the spiritual realm.** Oh really? Yes, really. Satan, the prince of darkness and his host do not have access to the hidden mysteries of God. If he did he could reveal God's mysteries to whomever he likes for his own evil purposes. Think about it. If the devil knew the hidden mysteries of God, no one would need to go to God to find out, everyone could go to Hell! But God is the God of all wisdom, so no; the devil does not know the hidden things of God. It is **ENCRYPTED**, protected even from the host of darkness (1Cor 2:6-8).

For where there is unbelief redemption cannot take place. So has God determined that some people will hear his word and turn to salvation and some not be converted because they cannot understand? I'm glad you asked.

There are two groups of people, those who can understand and perceive and those who cannot understand or perceive. Those who can understand and perceive have a choice to believe or reject Christ; to inherit promise or eternal damnation.

It is written *"Jacob have I loved, but Esau have I hated"* (Rom 9:13). Is God a partial, wicked, unrighteous God? No, but He however being the just, all-powerful, all-seeing God of infinite wisdom; who knows the end from the beginning of time, can decide to have mercy on one and not another, to have compassion on one and not another, to harden the heart of one and glorify Himself by the damnation of such a one or to glorify himself by blessing another.

We don't get to question God regarding His decision to do one thing or another. The clay does not have the choice to say to the potter what vessel it desires to be formed into. It is totally in the hands of the potter. The clay's best decision is to submit to the workings of the potter. So it is the Lord who hath made us. We did not make ourselves. We do not know what God wants to accomplish, we are not His advisors. He made all things for himself, even the wicked for the day of evil. (Isa 40:13, Rom 11:34)

For the scripture saith unto Pharaoh, Even for this same purpose have I raised thee up, that I might shew my power in thee, and that my name might be declared throughout all the earth. Rom 9:17

And the Lord said unto Moses, When thou goest to return into Egypt, see that thou do all those wonders before Pharaoh, which I have put in thine hand: but I will harden his heart, that he shall not let the people go. Ex 4:21

And I will harden Pharaoh's heart, and multiply my signs and my wonders in the land of Egypt. Ex 7:3

And I will harden Pharaoh's heart that he shall follow after them; and I will be honoured upon Pharaoh, and upon all his host; that the Egyptians may know that I am the Lord. Ex 14:4

The almighty God who is all-knowing, from the beginning of time had foreknowledge of those who would believe on His Son Jesus Christ *(The Lord is good, a strong hold in the day of trouble; and he knoweth them that trust in him* Nah 1:7*).*

He appointed those who would believe beforehand, before they were even conceived, to have the nature of Christ in them. He also gave them an inherent desire to change and constantly aspire to be like Christ, so that eventually they would acquire the spiritual image of the Son of God. These people who He appointed, He also called (named, identified as His and designated for a particular purpose) this being works finished (a purpose established) from the foundation of the world. Such He also justified (that is, vindicated, forgave and brought into good standing with Himself, sanctified for that purpose) so that they will be glorified having attained the image of Jesus Christ (Rom 8:28-31).

The essence of the matter is -

"[19]...The Lord knoweth them that are his... [20] But in a great house there are not only vessels of gold and of silver, but also of wood and of earth; and some to honour, and some to dishonour. [21] If a man therefore purge himself from these, he shall be a vessel unto honour, sanctified, and meet for the master's use, and prepared unto every good work". (2 Tim 2:19-21)

It is said therefore, "he that hath ears to hear, let him hear." (Matt 11:15). This admonition is given, because not everyone that hears can hear and understand. So if you can hear and understand you have a responsibility to choose unto salvation or damnation. Wow! Think about that.

Once we have been chosen by God, it is a privilege given forever. When chosen we are designated for eternal life and God holds us and protects us in the palm of his hand. We can walk away from his hand but no one not even the devil can take us away from Him. He will not send us away; we part only if we choose to leave.

25 Jesus answered, "I did tell you, but you do not believe. The miracles I do in my Father's name speak for me, 26 but you do not believe because you are not my sheep. 27 My sheep listen to my voice; I know them, and they follow me. 28 I give them eternal life, and they shall never perish; no one can snatch them out of my hand. 29 My Father, who has given them to me, is greater than all; no one can snatch them out of my Father's hand. 30 I and the Father are one." (John 10:25-30 NIV)

Immediately when we believe in Christ we are marked by the Holy Spirit as God's property. At that point "21He anointed us, 22set his seal of ownership on us, and put his Spirit in our hearts as a deposit, guaranteeing what is to come". (2 Cor. 1:21-22 NIV) God places his spirit in our hearts because the heart is the seat of belief. With the heart man believes unto righteousness (Rom 10:10). God looks at the heart. **We are marked as His when we believe, we accept his salvation when we confess that belief.**

[11] In him we were also chosen, having been predestined... [13] And you also were included in Christ when you heard the word of truth, the gospel of your salvation. Having believed, you were marked in him with a seal, the promised Holy Spirit, [14] who is a deposit guaranteeing our inheritance until the redemption of those who are God's possession - to the praise of his glory. Eph 1:11-14 NIV

When the Gentiles heard this, they were glad and honored the word of the Lord; and all who were appointed for eternal life believed. Acts 13:48 NIV

God functions as He declares and does not need to apologize or justify what He does to anyone. He is the potter who makes one vessel unto honor and another to dishonor.

Nuggets – God's Sweetness Not Weakness

1. God is the all-loving, all-powerful and impartial God.
2. He is also the powerful God of horrendous possibilities.
3. God's work is done on a level designed to cause fear in the heart of man because He wants worship.
4. God makes his chosen ones the centre of His attention and requires that we make Him the centre of our attention. He is a jealous GOD.
5. We cannot hinder God's pleasure. He will gain the pleasure he seeks from blessing us or destroying us.
6. God chooses whom He will favour. Everyone cannot be your favourite, you must choose.
7. Being chosen by God comes with privileges and responsibilities.
8. Now there is a new and better covenant.
9. Each person must believe on the Lord Jesus Christ in order to be saved.

OUR SPIRITUAL SERVERS

Serve Until They Become Word

The Christian journey is about growing into the nature of Christ, so that as Christ is **WORD** we become **WORD**. The human nature however, is antagonistic towards God and does not desire to be controlled by the laws of God; as such the journey is one of constant battles. The Christian must grow by building himself or herself in the **WORD**. Knowing that we wrestle not against flesh and blood we must be armed for battle as stipulated in Ephesians 6:11-18.

Also, as we seek to grow in spiritual stature, the challenge we face is not whether we are too small to defeat the adversary but have we grown big enough to accept that we cannot defeat him on our own.

Recognizing we need God's help and developing a habit of constantly depending on God to guide us daily, not only guarantees our success but sees us relinquishing all Glory to God. There is nothing more enchanting to God, all He craves is glory. **He wants bragging rights for everything that is manifested in the life of the believer. The more we are open to give Him Glory for what happens in our life, the more He is willing to show-up and manifest His awesome works on our behalf knowing that he will be magnified in the end.** Until we become **WORD**, God knows we need help. He has therefore made available at the request of Jesus Christ, the Holy Spirit to be our comforter, helper, counsellor, advocate, intercessor, and enabler. The

Holy Spirit will work with us and on our behalf, to ensure that we become all God desires of us.

The Holy Spirit, the comforter, comes as helper or **OUR SERVER** (analogous to computer server), a central point through which data is accessed, processed or may be stored. Jesus said: I am the way the truth and the life no man comes to the Father but by me (John 14:6). He also said If you ask anything in my name, I will do it (John 14:14) and If you ask of the Father anything in my name He will give it to you (John 16:23). In other words, **I am the one you must access or process all things through, I am your SERVER.**

The term server is very broadly used in information technology. Server may be used to describe many versions of hardware or software systems. Generally speaking, a server is a computerized operation wherein a resource is shared with one or more client processes. Server indicates a relationship where one part of a system provides service for a defined network of beneficiaries.

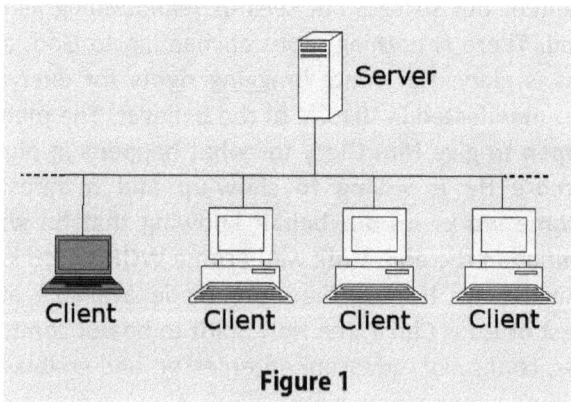

Figure 1

Bear in mind that it is possible for a unit to be both a server and a client, just as a person can be a doctor and also a patient.

As promised (John 14:26), Jesus sends us the comforter, the mighty Paraclētus, literally meaning the person called in to help us; or serve us, **OUR SERVER**, the Holy Spirit. When Jesus was leaving earth he promised he would send us, someone in his stead another comforter, intercessor, helper; **another SERVER**; someone who would represent him Christ here on earth. The Holy Spirit facilitates or assists the process of us receiving in our lives that which God desires for us and that which we communicate through Christ to God the Father.

The Greek word Paraclete translates as, comforter, advocate, intercessor, teacher, and helper, and it is a designation of the Holy Ghost. After Jesus ascended into heaven, the Paraclete was assigned the mission to abide with the disciples to be a continual representation of Christ with them, teaching them as He did when He dwelt among them as flesh, and bearing witness of the things which He then taught. Every dimension of spiritual function and every aspect of our salvation would be entrenched in the role of the Holy Spirit. He would execute His duty to ensure that the believer had all that is required, in resource, guidance, counsel and support so that we can mature and be ready for the coming of the Lord Jesus. In the meanwhile, the Holy Spirit also functions as a minister and further witness of Jesus on the earth, he dwells in us and enables us.(Romans 8:9, 11;1 Corinthians 3:16).

Do take care to note that some of the translations of the role of the Paraclete, such as advocate and intercessor, are similar to the role Jesus left earth to go and carry out in heaven on behalf of the believer.

So we have Jesus our advocate or SERVER in heaven and the Holy Spirit our SERVER dwelling in us here on earth. We therefore have two spiritual SERVERS.

When one hears the term **SERVER**, the name right off the bat conveys, service; doing something on another's behalf. In the context of computers there are many types of servers, among them are those referred to as client-servers. A client-server is a model with two components, client systems and server systems. Client and server systems may be configured to form a network that connects multiple users and allows interaction with each other. Every believer of Christ is a part of a network, the body of Christ (...for we are all members of one body." Eph 4:25). As members of this network it is expected that we:

- Serve one another in love. (Gal 5:13 NIV)
- Let the word of Christ dwell in us richly in all wisdom; teaching and admonishing one another in psalms and hymns and spiritual songs. (Col 3:16)
- Are full of goodness, complete in knowledge and competent to instruct one another.(Rom 15:14 NIV)
- Comfort ourselves together, and edify one another.(1Th 5:11)
- Provoke one another unto love and to good works (Heb 10:24)

- [1]Who are strong should bear with the failures of the weak and not only seek to please ourselves. [2]Each of us should please his neighbour and look out for his well-being so that we build him up. (Rom 15:1-2 NIV)

As believers we are also in constant interaction with The Holy Spirit the Server who dwells in us, and with Jesus Christ our server in heaven through whom we access whatever we request from God the Father. Jesus sent the Holy Spirit to reside in the believer and in so doing made precise and expeditious, communication by the believer to God. The Holy Spirit, a **SERVER**, the Word (logos) in the believer, operates as in Heb 4:12 (NIV) which depicts:

...the word of God is living and active. Sharper than any double-edged sword, it penetrates even to dividing soul and spirit, joints and marrow; it judges the thoughts and attitudes of the heart.

Before we pray to God, even while we are praying to God, the Holy Spirit is discerning the thoughts and intents of our heart and in conjunction with Jesus Christ advocates with God on our behalf, so that even while we are still praying God can answer that prayer. Think about how cookies on your computer work, you may be browsing the Internet looking at cars, doing your research so that you can know how to talk to a dealership when you go in. While you are still doing your research, messages are already popping up on your screen with advertisements from dealerships or other car related businesses in your own neighbourhood. The cookies stored on your computer by the server you are using allow information to be communicated regarding your interests. If man can figure out a way to respond to your needs that quickly, consider God's capacity to do greater.

God's **SERVERS**, Jesus and the Holy Spirit function on behalf of "clients" you and I, your spirit and my spirit, to enable our request made known to God, through prayer and sometimes through groaning of the spirit, to be fulfilled (Ex 2:24-25).

We do not always know what to pray. Sometimes the circumstance we encounter is way beyond us (it would seem, for God does not give us more than we can bear, and with every temptation gives us what we need so we are able to bear it (1Cor. 10:13)). We need help sometimes to fathom how to function in our circumstance. In such times the mighty Paraclete, the Holy Spirit, comes alongside us to help our infirmities; **he understands that we do not know what to pray and so he makes intercession for us with groaning which cannot be heard.** He searches and knows what is in our mind and our spirit and intercedes with God for us in agreement with the mind of God. This is the fulfilment of the promise of Jesus. When He was about to leave the earth he told his disciples *"the comforter which is the Holy Spirit whom the Father will send in my name shall teach you all things and bring all things to your* *remembrance, whatsoever I have said unto you" ((John 14:26)* [17] related references).

So one **SERVER**, the Holy Spirit that dwells in us here on earth makes requests, intercedes for us and helps us to receive from God. We also have a High Priest another **SERVER** who is holy, harmless, undefiled, separate from sinners, and made higher than the heavens. Jesus Christ, who does not need to on a daily basis offer up sacrifice first for his own sins, and then for the people's. Such a requirement had to be fulfilled by those high priests that functioned under the law. Jesus made His sacrifice once, when he offered up himself as the lamb slain for the sins of the world, atonement for eternity (Heb 7:26-27). He also intercedes for us from His throne at the right hand of the father. This **SERVER** can be touched with the feeling of our infirmities because He was in every regard tested as we

---

[17] *26 Likewise the Spirit also helpeth our infirmities: for we know not what we should pray for as we ought: but the Spirit itself maketh intercession for us with groanings which cannot be uttered. 27 And he that searcheth the hearts knoweth what is the mind of the Spirit, because he maketh intercession for the saints according to the will of God. Roman 8:26-27*

Lord, all my desire is before thee; and my groaning is not hid from thee. Ps 38:9

32 Then when Mary was come where Jesus was, and saw him, she fell down at his feet, saying unto him, Lord, if thou hadst been here, my brother had not died. 33 When Jesus therefore saw her weeping, and the Jews also weeping which came with her, he groaned in the spirit, and was troubled, 38 Jesus therefore again groaning in himself cometh to the grave. It was a cave, and a stone lay upon it. John 11:32-33, 38

are and came through with an impeccable record of purity. ([18]Related references)

He was despised and rejected of men; a man of sorrows, and acquainted with grief (Isa 53:3). Christ can represent us better than anyone else could because he can relate to our encounters.

Computer servers sometimes have downtime but there is no downtime with our SERVERS. We have two reliable SERVERS constantly processing our request, interceding for us, always working on our behalf. You know how sometimes you try to access a website and obtain error messages such as:

---

[18] *[31] What shall we then say to these things? If God be for us, who can be against us? [32] He that spared not his own Son, but delivered him up for us all, how shall he not with him also freely give us all things? [33] Who shall lay any thing to the charge of God's elect? It is God that justifieth. [34] Who is he that condemneth? It is Christ that died, yea rather, that is risen again, who is even at the right hand of God, who also maketh intercession for us. Rom 8:31-34*

[14] *Seeing then that we have a great high priest, that is passed into the heavens, Jesus the Son of God, let us hold fast our profession. [15] For we have not an high priest which cannot be touched with the feeling of our infirmities; but was in all points tempted like as we are, yet without sin. [16] Let us therefore come boldly unto the throne of grace, that we may obtain mercy, and find grace to help in time of need. Heb 4:14-16*

Error Message	Interpretation
Host unavailable	Host server down. Hit reload or go to the server later
Network connection refused by server	The web server is busy
500 Internal Error	Could not retrieve the website document because of server-configuration problems. Contact site administrator.
501 Not implemented	Wed server does not support a requested feature.
502 Service temporarily overloaded	Server congestion; too many connections;high traffic. Keep trying until the page reloads.
503 Service unavailable	Server busy, site may have moved, or you lost your dial-up internet connection.
Unable to locate Host	Host server is down, Internet connection is lost, or URL typed incorrectly.

Can you imagine needing help from God, getting down on your knees to pray and as you start to pray you hear "Holy Ghost unavailable, try praying later." Or being in a natural disaster and you try praying and get a 502 error message: "Service temporarily overloaded". **Our God is available to us limitlessly, and for free.** Moreover, He guarantees that we reach him when we call and our **SERVERS** ensure God

---

understands what we need when we call. When through prayer and supplication we make our request known to God, the **SERVERS** ensure it is processed and we obtain an answer in time.

If you are or have been exposed to a loving parent you have evidenced this played out day after day. We give our children cell phones and tell them, I want you to call me anytime you need me. If anything happens call me right away. We want to make sure that they are safe and no matter what we are attending to, they are our priority. We consider this modern parenting, but look; God already had such a system in place for His children. He said call me and I will answer you and tell you about great and mighty things that you have no clue about. And in fact before you call I will answer and while you are talking, I will still be listening[20]. Our **SERVERS** know the intents of our hearts and are connected with our spirit. They can intercede on our behalf before we even open our mouth. When we open our mouth it is an expression of faith but not to inform God about anything. "For with the heart man believeth unto righteousness; and with the mouth confession is made unto salvation (Rom 10:10).

---

[20] *Call unto me, and I will answer thee, and shew thee great and mighty things, which thou knowest not. Jer 33:3*

And it shall come to pass, that before they call, I will answer; and while they are yet speaking, I will hear. Isa 65:24

He shall call upon me, and I will answer him: I will be with him in trouble; I will deliver him, and honour him. Ps 91:15

God already knows everything, even what you are thinking you need to tell Him.

Priceless

Sometimes what is free is scoffed at or despised. We like to differentiate ourselves and often think we can show who is better by who can afford the best. Nonetheless, the old principle still stands that "the best things in life are free". It is said you get what you pay for, but salvation and the access it provides to the resources of God are free because none of us could afford to buy it. Salvation is not cheap, but it is free. Someone paid for it with His life, so it is free to us, because it is the greatest gift ever given to anyone (John 3:16). To despise God's grace and treat it with nonchalance is inexplicable ingratitude. Sometimes we behave in a manner that suggests that we really don't get it. We really do not understand that our bodies are the temple of the Holy Ghost? That the Holy Ghost lives in us? We often seem to slight the fact that such is the design of God, and we are not our own. We are bought with a price, our bodies and our spirits belong to God and so to glorify him in them is the only reasonable thing to do. (1Cor. 6:19-20)

Have you ever gone out of your way and at considerable cost obtained a gift for someone, which in your best judgment would bring them great benefit. Have you felt the heartbreak it brings to see that gift tossed aside with disregard because something else was desired? Often, not an item more important or beneficial, just something their emotions required for momentary fulfilment. God knows what is best for us and has gone to great length when He gave his only begotten son, so we could be redeemed. Some have pushed salvation aside for wealth, fame, hanging with the popular crowd or hanging with a desired girl or boy. Many have not taken the time to look closely enough at the gift, to see it includes all the guarantees we need for a fulfilled life, one of great joy and happiness, a purpose filled life and ultimately guaranteed eternal life.

Our redemption which was bought by Christ comes with two SERVERS to ensure support and guarantees among many things, that:

- **No GOOD THING** will God withhold from them that walk uprightly (Ps 84:11).
- They that seek the Lord **SHALL NOT WANT ANY GOOD THING** (Ps 34:9-10).
- God shall supply **ALL OUR NEED** according to His riches in glory by Christ Jesus (Phil 4:19).
- Our heavenly Father knows that we have need of these things but if we seek first the kingdom of God, and his righteousness; **ALL THESE THINGS** shall be added unto us (Matt 6:32-33).

- If we abide in Christ, and his words abide in us, we shall ask **WHAT WE WILL**, and it shall be done unto us (John 15:7).
- If we delight ourselves in the Lord, He shall give us **THE DESIRES OF OUR HEART** (Ps 37:4;Mark 11:24)
- **ALL THINGS**, whatsoever we shall ask in prayer believing, we shall receive (Mt 21:22).
- **NO EVIL SHALL BEFALL US**; neither shall any plague come near our dwelling (Ps 91:10).

- If we fear the Lord, and depart from evil, it shall be **HEALTH** to our navel, and marrow to our bones (Pr 3:7-8).
- **HAPPY** is that people, whose God is the Lord (Ps 144:15).

Multifaceted Servers

There are several types of client-server architecture. One type of architecture is the Two Tier Architecture, where a client is directly connected to a server. The Two Tier Architecture has some limitations which are overcome by introducing one or more middle tiers into the model. Introduction of the middle tier(s) allows clients to connect directly to a server that is responsible for processing the request for any of various types of services needed and as such obtain faster response times.

A server may be configured to carry out a single type of service, such as a database server, file server, print server, mail server or web server. On the other hand a server may be setup to perform more than one computing service. As such it may work as a database server and a mail server. **Our spiritual SERVERS are multifaceted, multifunctional and operate in complete agreement with the mind of God our source of complete and accurate information.** In communications lingo I guess we could say; **our spiritual SERVERS are always on the same wavelength.** The servers bring to us God's response as healer, provider, strength, peace and so on, according to our needs and for the fulfilment of God's promises to us.

Consider a couple that has lived together for many years, they have shared many ups and downs. Over time they begin to think alike and express themselves alike, they even begin to look alike. As time goes by they begin to open their mouths at the same time to utter the same words when encountering certain situations. Flip to an identical twin of the same sex, sharing time together in the womb. They are born and grow together, develop the same taste in food and dress. And in some cases they find they have significantly the same likes and dislikes. They care for each other and feel deeply each other's pain. If they are apart, one can sometimes tell if the other is in trouble. They function in a similitude that baffles human comprehension.

Along the same lines, twenty-two people, divided equally between male and female, participated in a study. They were asked to judge the looks, personalities and ages of 160 married couples. The participants viewed photographs of men and women separately and were not told who was married to whom. The subjects consistently judged people who were married as being similar in appearance and personality. The researchers also found that couples who had been together longer appeared more similar.[21]

The Holy Triad, has been together before the beginning of this world, created the universe together (let us make man), dwell together, share and sacrifice together for a cause. Is it strange that they as three (Spirit) persons function as one? If for nothing else, the passage of time together seems to make room for such a phenomenon;

---

[21] Personality and Individual Differences - March 2006 issue

that God the Father, Son and Holy Spirit can function as one in total agreement knowing each other's mind. There is however, much more to the unity of the Godhead than this. **SERVERS** have the responsibility to ensure that requests are processed and responses are delivered efficiently and effectively. Hence Jehovah God manifests His functional diversity as our banner, provider, healer, and so on, all administered through Jesus Christ and the Holy Spirit who intercede on our behalf and deliver our answers as:

Jehovah-Rophe: Healer - [4] *Surely he hath borne our griefs, and carried our sorrows: yet we did esteem him stricken, smitten of God, and afflicted.* [5] *But he was wounded for our transgressions; he was bruised for our iniquities: the chastisement of our peace was upon him; and with his stripes we are healed (Isa 53:4-5).*

Jehovah-Nissi: Banner - [11] *Thine, O Lord, is the greatness, and the power, and the glory, and the victory, and the majesty: for all that is in the heaven and in the earth is thine; thine is the kingdom, O Lord, and thou art exalted as head above all.* [12] *Both riches and honour come of thee, and thou reignest over all; and in thine hand is power and might; and in thine hand it is to make great, and to give strength unto all.* [13] *Now therefore, our God, we thank thee, and praise thy glorious name (I Chronicles 29:11-13).*

Jehovah-Shammah: Present with us - *Let your conversation be without covetousness; and be content with such things as ye have: for he hath said, I will never leave thee, nor forsake thee (Hebrews 13:5).*

Jehovah-Ganan: Lord Our Defence - *For the Lord is our defence; and the Holy One of Israel is our king (Ps 89:18).*

Jehovah-Gador Milchamah - Mighty in Battle - *Who is this King of glory? The Lord strong and mighty, the Lord mighty in battle (Ps 24:8).*
Jehovah-Jireh: Provider - *But my God shall supply all your need according to his riches in glory by Christ Jesus (Philip 4:19).*

Jehovah-Magen: Lord my Shield - *Happy art thou, O Israel: who is like unto thee, O people saved by the Lord, the shield of thy help, and who is the sword of thy excellency! and thine enemies shall be found liars unto thee; and thou shalt tread upon their high places (Deut 33:29).*

Jehovah-Shalom: Peace - *For unto us a child is born, unto us a son is given: and the government shall be upon his shoulder: and his name shall be called Wonderful, Counsellor, The mighty God, The everlasting Father, The Prince of Peace (Isa 9:6).*

[31] What shall we then say to these things? If God be for us, who can be against us? [32] He that spared not his own Son, but delivered him up for us all, how shall he not with him also freely give us all things? [33] Who shall lay any thing to the charge of God's elect? It is God that justifieth. [34] Who is he that condemneth? It is Christ that died, yea rather, that is risen again, who is even at the right hand of God, who also market intercession for us. [35] Who shall separate us from the love of Christ? shall tribulation, or distress, or persecution, or famine, or nakedness, or peril, or sword? (Rom 8:31-35).

Jehovah-Go'el - Lord My Redeemer - *And I will feed them that oppress thee with their own flesh; and they shall be drunken with their own blood, as with sweet wine: and all flesh shall know that I the Lord am thy Saviour and thy Redeemer, the mighty One of Jacob (Isa 49:26).*

Thou shalt also suck the milk of the Gentiles, and shalt suck the breast of kings: and thou shalt know that I the Lord am thy Saviour and thy Redeemer, the mighty One of Jacob (Isa 60:16).

Believers are able to see the fullness of the Godhead operating as one in us through us and on behalf of us. This is the privilege available through the connectivity we have with Christ and the Holy Spirit and the access provided to God the Father. Whatever the circumstance in which we find ourselves and whatever our need God will prove to be relevant and present, the I Am whatever we need right there and then. What God provides as answer to our prayer may not arrive when we thought it should, it may not look or feel like we expected or would have liked but he knows that what he delivers is right for us at that time.

Nuggets: Our Spiritual Servers

1. We have Jesus our advocate or SERVER in heaven and the Holy Spirit our SERVER dwelling in us here on earth.
2. Our servers help us communicate what is in our mind and our spirit to God and facilitates response from God.
3. We have two reliable servers constantly processing our request, interceding for us, always working on our behalf.
4. God already knows everything, even what you're thinking you need to tell Him.
5. Our spiritual SERVERS are multifaceted, multifunctional and operate in complete agreement with the mind of God.

THE ENCRYPTED WORD SENT TO GOD

A Personal Gift

We have so far discussed the fact that God has encrypted His word to those who believe in Him. Noteworthy as well, is that God has also provided for our communication to him to be encrypted. It makes sense that God would provide for us to communicate with Him in an encrypted manner. Consider that if God's message to us is encrypted (coded) but our communication to Him is unencrypted (not encode), the conversation becomes open to others at that point and the privacy of the conversation would be lost. Available as one of God's spiritual gifts (1Cor 12:8-10, Eph 4:7-13, Rom 12:3-8) is the gift of the unknown tongue (also referred to as the gift of speaking in tongues). This gift allows the believer to speak to God in mysteries just as He is able to speak to the believer in mysteries.

Paul in 1 Cor. 12:31 admonished the church to strive for the greater spiritual gifts. Evidently, the believer can have more than one spiritual gift. All the gifts of the spirit are given by God functioning through the Holy Ghost. Some gifts were also highlighted by Paul as greater and some lesser gifts; some for personal profit and some for the profit of the church as a body of believers. Paul also took the time to note however, that the manifestation of the Spirit is given to every man for profit (1 Cor. 12:7). Therefore, whether it is a greater or lesser gift, all gifts from God are profitable, they are beneficial. The context of this book will be confined to examine the gift of speaking in unknown tongues. Paul in his teachings to the Corinthian Church noted:

....he that speaketh in an unknown tongue speaketh not unto men, but unto God: for no man understandeth him; howbeit in the spirit he speaketh mysteries (1Cor 14:2).

It was discussed earlier in this book that God encrypts the mysteries of His kingdom and reveals such mysteries to them who are His. The Holy Spirit decodes the encrypted word to the believer. In 1Cor 14:2 Paul outlines that the believer can also speak mysteries to God, even though those around may hear and not understand a single word of the dialogue taking place. He goes on to explain that:

[4] He that speaketh in an unknown tongue edifieth himself; but he that prophesieth edifieth the church. [5] I would that ye all spake with tongues..., 1Cor 14: 4-5

The gift of speaking in an unknown tongue provides for an **ENCRYPTED** conversation between the believer and God. Through the exercise of this gift the believer's individual life can be significantly strengthened. He communicates from his spirit to God and God downloads hidden secrets in the believer's spirit. When Jesus was present on earth He was the teacher and He taught in parables **(encryption)** in order that the disciples would know the mysteries concerning the kingdom of Heaven but others would not. When he was leaving He promised to send another comforter who would teach us all things. Now, that comforter, the Holy Spirit, teaches us the mysteries of God, encrypted so only the believer can hear and understand and see and perceive the hidden things of God (Matt 13:11).

Each of us has been given a gift(s) for our benefit and that of the body of Christ. Paul points out:

1. God has given every person the measure of faith (Rom 12:3).

This is important because we believe by faith. Belief is the foundation of our relationship with God.

> **Our belief is fuelled by our faith, which means that faith drives the extent to which we believe.**

Each gift of God is available to every child of God. We can only receive any gift from God if we believe, and that requires faith.

We receive faith by hearing God's message (Rom 10:17-18 NIV). Hearing is not just about auditory ability. Hearing is connected to the ability to understand the message to which we are exposed. God has already given the believer the ability to hear and understand. We cannot understand the message of Christ if we have never heard (or been exposed to) it. Herein therefore lies the element of human responsibility, we can study God's word; we can put ourselves in circumstances where we hear his message in order that faith may be nourished, as in doing so we build our faith by increasing our knowledge and understanding of God's word.

Do we need more faith to enable us to do more? I guess not, because faith is not about how much but how strong. The disciples asked Jesus once to increase their faith; his response to them was: "if you have faith as a mustard seed you can move mountains" (Matt 17:20). The measure of faith given by God is sufficient for all our needs. Faith is developed somewhat like a muscle. We are born with muscle tissue. One person during growth eats and exercises in a manner that is healthy for the body and builds strong muscle. The muscle becomes bigger and stronger the more it is nourished and exercised. In its developed state the muscle can show off great form and beauty, move great masses, twist and turn things the feeble cannot even imagine possible. Generally speaking we are all endowed with the same capability but only those who tend rightly to that potential given will see its manifest strength. Those who do not exercise their muscle may never even know its capability. As it is in the natural so it is in the spiritual. We all have been given the measure of faith by God. By exercising our faith and feeding on God's word we are able to see the wonders resultant of great faith. Faith comes by the word but faith without works is dead. It is not new faith or more faith that brings results; rather it is **fit faith**. Faith fit to manage any circumstance that we encounter.

If we have faith as a mustard seed, that's all the faith we will ever need because we have that

which we can exercise and build to move mountains.

One can develop muscle atrophy, where often due to lack of use, injury or disease, the inactive muscle shrinks, becomes weak and waste away. In similitude, faith without works is dead (James 2:20), inactive faith will waste away. A muscle will not in the atrophic state carry out its intended function, the muscle tissue is there, it is just too weak to do anything. The atrophic state of the muscle lessens or weakens its ability to function. In order for that muscle to regain normal functionality it will have to be nurtured with the right care, food and exercise. Faith is similar; lack of use lessens or weakens its ability to function. We must exercise our faith; it is the only way to please God. Do you believe in God? ...then you have faith (1Peter 1:9) (Heb 11:6). Have you ever trusted him to come through for anything and saw that He did? ...then you know your faith works. Muscle atrophy is caused by disease, injury or lack of use. "Faith atrophy" is caused by the same things. Jesus said I have prayed for you that your faith will not fail (ref. Luke 22:31-32). It is imperative that we exercise our faith and also guard our faith against disease, any influence that could create "dis ease" in the use or functioning of our faith. The prefix "dis" indicates the lack, removal or negation of something. Therefore anything that:

- seeks to rob you of your faith,
- imposes on you the sense that you cannot

function with faith,
- induces in you the sense that you have no faith,
is spiritually destructive.

Faith is diametrically opposed to reason. We cannot reason how that which is related to our belief will manifest or operate. Our job is to declare that the thing which we desire is, and faith is displayed when we speak and function in conformity to the affirmation of that which we have declared.

You must take care then that no force convinces you that what God has done is a coincidence or that it is the result of anything other than you know is the truth of your encounter; which is, you believed God and He brought fulfilment in your circumstance. You should guard against injury from those who would castigate your spiritual standing or with their tongue try to crush your faith. When God comes through for you, attribute the result to Him, trust and believe Him continually for more and greater things temporal and spiritual needs alike. Eventually nothing can question your faith; you will have seen God work enough times, in big enough ways for you to know without hesitation that your faith works. This is how we survive, for the just can only live by faith (Heb 6:1). (See also Heb 11). Having a fit faith is how we can maximize that which God has for us and Jude 20 tells us how:

²⁰ But ye, beloved, building up yourselves on your most holy faith, praying in the Holy Ghost. Jude 20

The essence of Jude's instruction is that we build ourselves in the most holy faith through the knowledge of God's word. And when exposed to the word, praying in the Holy Ghost brings the revelation embodied in the word we have studied as relevant to our individual life and circumstance.

So how does faith work? What is this faith?

Faith is the **substance of** things hoped for, the **evidence** of things not seen (Heb 11:1). Remember earlier in the section of this book entitled "Word Power" we examined the power of God's Word. In that section we discussed that the rhema word is the **WORD** spoken that has potency to manifest in substantive form, a noun (person, place or thing). We examined that **uttered words have the power to be transformed into noun form, logos, being the word's substance** (physical form or something of evidential effect) **person, place or thing.**

Word and faith are intertwined at the heart of a functioning believer's life. Faith, being the substance and evidence of things we hope for and have not seen, comes by hearing the word. The word which is heard must be believed and evidence of belief is through utterance (From the abundance of the heart the mouth speaks). This is also why the Bible says to have salvation we must believe and then confess with our mouth. When we hear God's word and we believe it, utterance, words then transform what we hear and believe into reality, hence the popular expression "speaking things into being".

It is worth mentioning that:

> **"God Principles"** will often work not just for believers, but for anyone who correctly applies the principle.

A person who does not believe in God but believes in the principle of faith whatever the name otherwise given to that principle, that person if they apply the principle will have the results.

I believe one of the things the gift of speaking in tongues does is it allows unhindered conversation with God so that clarity can be obtained by a person regarding anything the heart ponders. **Clarity of position on a matter enhances belief and allows greater focus.**

Paul also points out:

2. We should operate as members of one body

Diversity of gifts is present in the body of Christ and is necessary for the body of Christ to function as a whole.

Irrespective of other gifts endowed on a believer, the gift of speaking in an unknown tongue should not be despised. If you are a prophet, being able to communicate with God spirit to spirit will enrich your life so that you can be a better prophet. If you have the gift of healing, being able to communicate with God spirit to spirit will enrich your life in order that you can better function in that gift and so on.

The gift of speaking in tongues is for personal enrichment and enables one to more effectively serve through other gifts.

The gift of tongues was spoken of by Paul as a lesser gift in the context of its value to the church. Such that when one speaks in tongues, the group hears but does not understand unless there is interpretation. Interesting, here we see again the same context of hearing and not understanding; **ENCRYTED** dialogue. This is how God restricts access to others when He speaks to us. Here we see him giving us a gift whereby we can speak to him and others can hear and not understand; ummh what's He up to? Restricted access to others when we speak to Him?

In the natural some gifts are for the benefit of a group such as when at Christmas a gift is given to your family; but often the more treasured gifts are the ones given to you as an individual.

The gift of speaking in tongues is for individual advancement, for individual communication to God. We have access to an ENCRYPTED mode by which we can communicate with God; Spirit to Spirit. Thus facilitating a pure conversation where the truth of one's heart can be poured out to God, our father who art in heaven, without the limitations of words or language.

When we want to express ourselves, words can be a very limiting factor. This may be due to the boundary of our own vocabulary or the limits of a word's meaning within a particular context. We know that some of the essence of a conversation can get lost during translation from one language to another. At other times the emotion is just not conveyed by the spoken word. There is significant benefit when we are able to speak to God spirit to spirit as it removes such encumbrances.

We know further, that we are inept at translating our own true feelings. The Holy Spirit therefore helps our infirmities so we can communicate with God and convey with the deepest sincerity, the optimal expression of our soul (mind, emotions and will).

There are various examples of spiritual leaders whose prayer lives were significantly advanced in their time spent with God praying in the spirit. Paul himself in speaking says "I speak in tongues more than you all" (1Cor 14:18). There are also accounts of many who did not have the gift of speaking in tongues but as they sought the Lord in prayer, have been endowed with this gift. Within the context of using the gift openly in church, it will not benefit others unless there is interpretation. Others will have no clue what you are praying about; and this is by design. The gift is your personal, private tool to deeply commune with God.

The epistle of Jude the brother of Christ is very short. It was written in an era when the church was up against hostile heresies. The intrusion of false teachers in local churches was prevalent. In this dire situation the Holy Spirit inspired

Jude to write warning the church of this threat and encouraging them. In this synoptic book, I believe Jude would have attempted to address the most salient issues related to the brethren's predicament. It therefore speaks volumes concerning the value to the believer which he places on the gift of speaking in tongues, when one takes notice that Jude, in this brief epistle to encourage the brethren, admonished that they build themselves up in the faith and praying in the Holy Spirit Jude 20-21.

Speaking in tongues is one of those things God reserves for the appointed ones; those who believe. It is a personal and precious gift that can serve to deepen our relationship with him.

Some persons have consistently focused on Paul's scolding of the church in Corinth and their use of tongues. Some have gone as far as to emphasize it being a lesser gift than all others. I believe to endorse such accounts is to neglect the observance of the context in which Paul's letter was written. The church meetings had become disorderly because of the misunderstanding of how to effectively use the gift of tongues. Also, Paul being an evangelist was keen on the non-believers being reached. The manner of conduct in the house at the time was not presenting Christianity and its various tenets in a way that would edify non-believers and attract them to embrace Christ.

Paul went on to write saying "thank God I speak in tongues more than you all", because he knew the personal value of the gift. His admonition to the Corinthian church was therefore for counsel to more effectively achieve the evangelical objective. In such context speaking in tongues was not the most effective tool. God is the giver of all good gifts (James 1:17). Paul further encouraged the Corinthian church: "Wherefore, brethren, covet to prophesy, and **forbid not** to speak with tongues" (1Cor 14:39).

To treat the gift of tongues as something that makes Christians look ridiculous and redundant is an insult to God. If you are a believer, it should be a foregone conclusion that nothing that God gives us is beneath us. If we do not understand the value of the gift with which we have been blessed we can ask God for enlightenment.

> **Not having the gift to speak in an unknown tongue does not indicate that a person is not a Christian. Having the gift however, does provide a tool for one to be a more effective Christian.**

Consider a scenario where you are given a cell phone device by the President of the USA. He considers you a close and trusted friend, like family. You are on his shortlist of persons who can call him anytime using this device. The device however, is programmed so you can only call one number, his number. Conversations are scrambled (encrypted) and can only be interpreted by you inputting a special password. You received the nicely wrapped gift from the President and open it. Like so many people, you have not bothered to read the instructions carefully because you know how to use a cell phone. So you charge the phone and away you go, trying to make calls to members of your old address book. Well imagine the resulting frustrations. Anyone looking on would think you don't have a clue how to operate a cell phone. Your attitude now is "this is a piece of junk! My old phone works better." Well it does, for what you are trying to do.

If you read the manual you would see, you have been given a custom device. Giving you access only few have, to the ears of the most powerful person in the world. Well, well. How were you supposed to know it's a different kind of cell phone? Ummh let's see. You trust the source; based on your relationship you know he would only give you something good. He would never make a fool out of you or embarrass you. He cares about you and therefore he wants you to be able to be in touch whenever you need to, or just want to.

How does one receive the gift of speaking in tongues? How does one receive any gift from God? The reality is that nothing is transacted with God without faith. It is by faith that all gifts are obtained from God. There are encounters in the Bible where persons needed to trust God in a manner, similar to that which we are called to exercise for the gift of speaking in tongues.

In one instance God desired to use Moses as His messenger to the Egyptians. Moses however thought that he was inept at speech and lacked confidence to serve God in the required capacity. God found it necessary to remind Moses that he was the master of everything including his ability to speak. So God said to Moses:

[11].... who makes man's mouth? Who makes the dumb, or deaf, the one who sees, or the blind? Is it not I the Lord who does? [12] Now get going, I will speak through your mouth, and instruct you what to declare at the right time. (Ex 4:11-12)

Jeremiah also had his own encounter, in that as a child, God chose to use him to prophesy to the Israelites regarding the recompense related to their idolatrous practices. Jeremiah accounts how the word of the Lord came to him saying:

[5] "Before I formed you in the womb I knew you, before you were born I set you apart; I appointed you as a prophet to the nations." [6] "Ah, Sovereign Lord," I said, "I do not know how to speak; I am only a child." [7] But the Lord said to me, "Do not say, 'I am only a child.' You must go to everyone I send you to and say whatever I command you. [8] Do not be afraid of them, for I am with you and will rescue you," declares the Lord.

[9] Then the Lord reached out his hand and touched my mouth and said to me, "Now, I have put my words in your mouth. [10] See, today I appoint you over nations and kingdoms to uproot and tear down, to destroy and overthrow, to build and to plant." (Jer 1:5-10 NIV)

The Lord gave further insight into his omnipotence when he pointed out to Israel

*I am the Lord your God, who brought you up out of Egypt.
Open wide your mouth and I will fill it. (Ps 81:10 NIV)*

The context of this statement was to assure Israel, that
even as God had previously provided for them in many
ways in the past, if they served him only as their true and
living God He would provide all their needs. This promise
spoke to a gesture tantamount to God's initial act of
breathing into man's nostrils a composite of his
embodiment to create a living soul. The enactment of this
promise would see God breathing into humankind, pouring
out of himself into them the resources for the enablement
or manifestation of anything they required to function in
honouring Him, be it in the form of an expression or
material provision.

Consequently, when approaching God for the gift of
tongues, prophesy or any gift, worship becomes pivotal.
Through sincere worship our spirit becomes open to God
and he then willingly pours out of himself into us. In this
posture, the Holy Spirit makes our desire known to God
and he fulfils the desire of the heart. We speak in tongues
as the Holy Spirit gives utterance. Without pride or
reasoning, in a state of worship we submit so the Holy
Spirit can teach us how to pray as a spirit, and we speak as
we obey.

Know God for Yourself

As we seek to advance in the things of God, we must listen keenly and take care to discern the voice of God in all matters. We must be always cognizant of the "Pharisee spirit" which speaks authoritatively of God but denies the power thereof. As such John wrote:

"Beloved, believe not every spirit, but try the spirits whether they are of God: because many false prophets are gone out into the world" (1 John 4:1).

The apostle Paul also wrote in his letter to Timothy:

*"[1] This know also, that in the last days perilous times shall come. [2] For men shall be lovers of their own selves, covetous, boasters, proud, blasphemers, disobedient to parents, unthankful, unholy, [3] Without natural affection, trucebreakers, false accusers, incontinent, fierce, despisers of those that are good, [4] Traitors, heady, highminded, lovers of pleasures more than lovers of God; [5] **Having a form of godliness, but denying the power thereof: from such turn away**"(2 Tim 3:1-5).*

Christians cannot afford to listen to the world regarding the things of God. Why would you listen to one who cannot see, to guide you concerning the perception of a thing they have never seen? Why would you rely on one to give you counsel on a thing of which they have never heard? We cannot rely on unbelievers to be our compass regarding the things of God because they cannot hear and cannot perceive the things of God. To be accepted by worldly standards, some approach the things of God with worldly thinking and end up being robbed of the mysteries God wants to give.

With Bible revisions, commentaries and theological literature exploding around us; be mindful that being able to hear from God for yourself; becomes even more important. Many are throwing in their own ideas and opinions but God has reserved the mysteries to download into the hearts of the believer directly, so there is no watering down, no error of interpretation. The gift of the unknown tongue allows direct communication with God in a manner that is unadulterated.

> **There is no greater investment in one's eternal destiny than to ensure that we have developed a proven relationship with God. It is important that we know when God is speaking.**

God invites us to test him (Mal 3:10), He knows no one in their right mind relies on anything that has not been tested and proven. Once we have tested and are satisfied with something, we expect it to function, we will not test it every time unless to do so is a requirement for normal use; otherwise we just use it.

More time spent communicating with God, gives him more opportunity to relate to us. As he communicates with us and we are obedient to him we find in Him a trustworthy proven relationship.

My mother used to say: **"My child you must know God for yourself."** Anyone who is able to read can read the Bible and express an opinion.

The real message is what is revealed in your spirit while you study God's word. The word is important, the mysteries behind the word is of much greater value.

Not everyone who reads receives the mysteries of God because the word is a discerner of the intent of the heart. **No one can con God into opening up His treasures.**

"[12] For the word of God is quick, and powerful, and sharper than any twoedged sword, piercing even to the dividing asunder of soul and spirit, and of the joints and marrow, and is a discerner of the thoughts and intents of the heart.[13] Neither is there any creature that is not manifest in his sight: but all things are naked and opened unto the eyes of him with whom we have to do" (Heb 4:12-13).

No wonder Jesus rejoiced in spirit and said:

"I thank thee, O Father, Lord of heaven and earth, that thou hast hid these things from the wise and prudent, *and hast revealed them unto babes: even so, Father; for so it seemed good in thy sight"* (Luke 10:21).

The heart must be right when we go to study God's word. Our knowledge does not impress God. **To impress God we must be humble like Job, so God can confidently boast; have you considered my servant Job?**

Making the Best of Your Time Together

If you are employed to a company and you are going to meet with your CEO, how do you go? If you are passing by his or her office and just knocked on the door for a quick hello, you take nothing with you. He or she may bid you in for a chat if the time is right; otherwise it is brief and you are on your way after a short exchange and maybe being given instructions, which you will make sure to note as you step back into your office.

If however, you have a scheduled business meeting with the CEO. You would turn up with your notepad, laptop or some device for making notes, and a mind ready to engage in discourse with this person. You know they will have many important things to bring to bear during your time in their presence. Any less may seem downright disrespectful. When we come to speak to God, do we just turn-up? Or are we prepared to take note of what He will say to us? Do we think anything of importance might transpire? Do we come to Him ready to engage? God is always ready to download powerful stuff into our spirit and to squander what He imparts is to be unprepared for his presence, to be slight regarding what this time is about.

We should not just come to talk to God, we should purpose in our hearts to come to Him and listen. He already knows what we have to say, so we can go ahead and say it. More importantly, we should listen, because what God has to say, we don't know yet.

God has given us the gift of speaking in tongues in order that we can share with him spirit to spirit. We can share the most sincere and intimate things any time we desire to and without anyone being able to eavesdrop. I thank Him for that opportunity. Now you know why Paul says I thank God I speak in tongues more than you all. You can be in the presence of the King twenty four hours a day, seven days a week because He loves spending time with you and having conversations with you. Further He doesn't think you have anything better to do, nor does He consider anything better for him to do. Well, I'll take *that* gift!

Nuggets: The Encrypted Word Sent To God

1. All gifts from God are profitable.
2. The gift of speaking in tongues is for individual advancement, and facilitates communication spirit to spirit. It removes the limiting factor of words or language.
3. Not everyone who reads the word receives the mystery in the word.
4. We should not just come to talk to God, but purpose in our hearts to listen to Him.
5. God has given every person a measure of faith.
6. Faith is diametrically opposed to reason.
7. "God Principles" will often work not just for believers, but for anyone who correctly applies the principle.
8. The gift of speaking in tongues is for personal enrichment and enables one to more effectively serve through other gifts.
9. Know God for yourself.